THE CIVIL WAR

VOLUME 5

= Home front, Confederate - Legacy of the Civil War =

GROLIER

Published 2004 by Grolier, an imprint of Scholastic Library Publishing
Sherman Turnpike
Danbury, Connecticut 06816

© 2004 The Brown Reference Group plc

Set ISBN: 0-7172-5883-1
Volume ISBN: 0-7172-5888-2

Library of Congress Cataloging-in-Publication Data
The Civil War
        p.cm.
    Includes bibliographical references (p.) and index.
    Contents: v. 1. Abolition–Camp followers—v. 2. Camp life–Custer,
George A.—v. 3. Daily Life–Flags—v. 4.Florida–Hill, Ambrose P.—v. 5.
Home front, Confederate–Legacy of the Civil War—v. 6. Lincoln,
Abraham–Mobile Bay, Battle of—v. 7. Money and Banking–Politics,
Confederate—v. 8. Politics, Union–Shenandoah Valley—v. 9. Sheridan,
Philip H.–Trade—v. 10. Training–Zouaves.

    ISBN 0-7172-5883-1 (set: alk paper)—ISBN 0-7172-5884-X (v.1: alk paper)—
ISBN 0-7172-5885-8 (v.2: alk paper)—ISBN 0-7172-5886-6 (v.3: alk paper)—
ISBN 0-7172-5887-4 (v.4: alk paper)—ISBN 0-7172-5888-2 (v.5: alk paper)—
ISBN 0-7172-5889-0 (v.6: alk paper)—ISBN 0-7172-5890-4 (v.7: alk paper)—
ISBN 0-7172-5891-2 (v.8: alk paper)—ISBN 0-7172-5892-0 (v.9: alk paper)—
ISBN 0-7172-5893-9 (v.10: alk paper)

    1. United States—History—Civil War, 1861–1865—Encyclopedias,
Juvenile. [United States—History—Civil War, 1861–1865—
Encyclopedias.] 1. Grolier (Firm)

    E468.C613 2004
    973.7'03—dc22

    2003049315

For information address the publisher:
Grolier
Sherman Turnpike,
Danbury, Connecticut 06816

FOR THE BROWN REFERENCE GROUP PLC
Project Editor: Emily Hill
Deputy Editor: Jane Scarsbrook
Designer: Paul Griffin
Picture Researcher: Becky Cox

Maps: David Atkinson
Indexer: Kay Ollerenshaw
Managing Editor: Tim Cooke
Consultants: Professor James I. Robertson Jr,
                Virginia Technical Institute and
                State University
            Dr. Harriet E. Amos Doss,
                University of Alabama in Birmingham

Printed and bound in Singapore

ABOUT THIS BOOK

The Civil War was one of the turning points in U.S. history. The bitter "War between Brothers" cast a shadow that reaches to the present day. For the North the war began in determination to preserve the Union and ended as a crusade to free the slaves. For the South the conflict was the inevitable result of tensions between state and federal power that some argue remain unresolved. In its cavalry charges and sieges the war echoed wars of previous centuries; in its rifled weapons and its huge casualty figures—an estimated 620,000 soldiers died in four years of fighting—it looked forward to the world wars of the 20th century. This set of 10 books tells the stories of the key events, individuals, and battles of the struggle that split the nation. The alphabetically arranged entries also cover the social and political context of the fighting, and describe the involvement of every state in the war.

The Civil War was the first widely photographed war, and most of the images in the set were taken during the conflict itself. Most of the illustrations are also from contemporary sources, including the "special artists" who were sent to depict the battle action by newspaper editors. There are also numerous boxes giving eyewitness descriptions of individuals' experiences in battle or on the home front. Each entry ends with a list of cross-references to entries on related subjects elsewhere in the set. They will enable you to follow the subjects you are interested in and build your knowledge. At the end of each book there is a useful further reading list that includes websites, a glossary of special terms, and an index covering all 10 volumes.

Text: Harriet Amos Doss, Charles Bowery, Cynthia
        Brandimarte, Tom Brown, Jacqueline Campbell,
        Gregg Cantrell, Chris Capozzola, Janet Coryell, Anita
        Dalal, Alan C. Downs, Larry Gara, Mark Grimsley,
        Anthony Hall, Tim Harris, Herman Hattaway, Edward
        Horton, R. Douglas Hurt, Ted Karamanski, Phil
        Katcher, Rachel Martin, Robert Myers, Henry
        Russell, John David Smith, Karen Utz, Chris Wiegand

Contents

Home front, Confederate

Southern civilians experienced the war in a much more immediate way than their Northern counterparts. The war was on their doorstep, even in their very homes, forever altering Southern lives.

In 1861 most Southerners welcomed the war with enthusiasm. They did not expect the wartime scarcities and hardships they would later have to endure, because they thought that the war would be short and the North quickly defeated. With three out of four eligible men serving in the Confederate army the Southern home front was largely a world of women, children, and slaves. As their men marched off to war, Confederate women threw themselves into activities such as sewing flags, raising money, and organizing hospitals and relief associations. Most women declared their willingness to make sacrifices for the Confederate cause and encouraged their men to do the same, shaming any man who showed reluctance to enlist immediately and fight for Southern independence.

Support for the cause

White Southerners of the elite planter class had an unwavering faith in the Confederate cause, which they maintained until the end of the war. They assumed that their own interests represented those of all Southerners. Many did not even consider that slaves

An 1864 etching by Adalbert Volck of Southern women spinning, weaving, and sewing to make clothes for Confederate soldiers.

A Northern engraving of 1863 entitled "Sowing and Reaping," showing Southern women persuading their husbands to go to war (left) and then suffering the later consequences of their actions (right): Dressed in rags, the desperate women riot for bread.

on their plantations might have a different stake in the outcome—or that there might be differences of opinion among whites. When some poorer white men showed reluctance to join the army, planter families concluded that it was a result of personal cowardice rather than political belief.

Women as managers

Women often had to take charge of family farms when their husbands and sons were away fighting, and plantation owners' wives had to run the plantations. Their husbands wrote letters full of agricultural advice about matters such as planting, harvesting, marketing, and negotiating relations with overseers and slaves. But the mail service was irregular, and effectively women were on their own. Some rose to the occasion, while others crumbled under increasing pressure.

Of all plantation duties it was usually slave management that most challenged planter-class women. Mistresses just did not command the same authority as masters. Slaves began to leave work undone, ignore orders, or run away to the Union lines. Planter women often found changes in their slaves' behavior difficult to grasp. Many could not, or would not, accept that slavery was ending and clung to the belief that slaves really were passive, faithful, and helpless, as whites had often imagined them to be.

Twenty Negro Law

Early in the war the Confederate authorities were sympathetic to the problems of unsupervised slaves. A law was passed that allowed any plantation with more than 20 slaves to have a white man—either a master or an overseer—exempted from duty as a soldier. Poorer families who did not have slaves and whose women were forced to labor in the fields themselves when their husbands were in the army

BUTLER'S PROCLAMATION

An outrageous insult to the Women of New Orleans!

Southern Men, avenge their wrongs !!!

Head-Quarters, Department of the Gulf, New Orleans, May 15, 1862.

General Orders, No. 28.

As the Officers and Soldiers of the United States have been subject to repeated insults from the women calling themselves ladies of New Orleans, in return for the most scrupulous non-interference and courtesy on our part, it is ordered that hereafter when any Female shall, by word, gesture, or movement, insult or show contempt for any officer or soldier of the United States, she shall be regarded and held liable to be treated as a woman of the town plying her avocation.

By command of Maj.-Gen. BUTLER,
GEORGE C. STRONG,
A. A. G. Chief of Staff

A Confederate poster protesting against Union General Benjamin Butler's Order 28. Butler, the occupying commander in New Orleans, ordered that any woman who insulted Union troops was to be treated as a prostitute.

1862, severely restricting the availability of vital goods. For example, there was a desperate need for salt to preserve meat. The South had imported most of its salt and was never able to develop enough domestic sources to satisfy demand. Iron for railroad tracks and locomotives had also been imported, so the South could not replace railroads destroyed by Union armies.

Leather shoes, manufactured cloth, and coffee were some of the other everyday goods that became

resented this favoring of the upper classes, especially as they struggled to provide for their own hungry families.

Southern shortages

The strain on Southern agriculture was enormous. Despite the conversion of thousands of acres of cotton to staple crops, by 1862 food shortages were severe. In many cases the problem was not insufficient food but the lack of an organized distribution system. Military shipments took priority on inadequate transportation systems, so food often rotted in warehouses while civilians went hungry. The Union blockade of Southern ports began to take effect in

BREAD RIOTS

Despite the Confederate government's best efforts, increasing desperation led to civilian protests across the South. By the spring of 1863 the last crops from the previous year's drought-ravaged season were running out. Prices spiraled out of control. A family's weekly grocery bill for staples such as flour and butter had risen from a prewar $6.55 to $68.25. Civilians suspected that storekeepers and the government were hoarding supplies, and in a dozen or more places starving women staged bread riots.

The worst of these riots occurred in Richmond, Virginia, where several hundred women—later joined by men and boys—began to smash store windows and seize food and clothing. Confederate President Jefferson Davis himself arrived on the scene to calm the rioters. But despite Davis's appeal to Southern patriotism, the crowd refused to leave. Eventually he warned them to go home or he would order the militia to fire, and the crowd dispersed.

increasingly scarce. People had to exercise their ingenuity to find substitutes. Many women took out their spinning wheels and made cloth, called "homespun," from which they sewed dresses. Several Southerners recorded in their diaries the pride they took in wearing homespun as a mark of their sacrifice for the war effort.

The hardships created by shortages were made worse by the growing worthlessness of the Confederate currency. Inflation, which saw prices rise more than sevenfold, put even basic foods beyond the reach of many.

Refugees

Although families in the countryside felt the pinch of shortages and inflated prices, they were better off than those in the increasingly crowded cities. Nevertheless many rural families whose homes and farms lay in the path of invading troops decided to flee. Only a month after the war began, many northern Virginians left their homes; by 1862 this trickle had become a flood.

In 1864 Ulysses S. Grant began to implement his plan to "squeeze the South" by marching his troops through the Confederacy with orders to destroy everything they found. Union General William T. Sherman's march through Georgia and the Carolinas sent more families fleeing. At least 250,000 Southerners became refugees. Most ended up in cities such as Richmond, Columbia, and Atlanta, placing increased demands on already inadequate supplies of housing, food, and public services.

Often there was chaos when large communities fled before an invading army. In Columbia, South Carolina, for example, the prewar population of

8,000 had risen to 24,000 by February 1865. When Sherman's arrival became imminent, there was great confusion as officials, military personnel, and civilians all rushed to leave. Stations were jammed with people trying to board trains. Some smashed windows in their frantic attempts to escape.

An illustration from Harper's Weekly of June 14, 1862, showing the starving citizens of New Orleans being fed by the Union military authorities after they captured the city.

SIEGE OF VICKSBURG

An extract from the diary of an anonymous lady in Vicksburg: "March 20th. The slow shelling of Vicksburg goes on all the time, and we have grown indifferent. It does not at present interrupt or interfere with daily avocations, but I suspect they are only getting the range of different points; and when they have them all, showers of shot will rain on us all at once. Noncombatants have been ordered to leave or prepare accordingly. Those who are to stay are having caves built. Cave-digging has become a regular business; prices range from $20 to $50. ... Two diggers worked at ours a week and charged $30. It is well made in the hill that slopes just in the rear of the house, and well propped with thick posts, as they all are. It has a shelf, also, for holding a light or water. When we went in this evening and sat down, the earthy, suffocating feeling, as of a living tomb, was dreadful to me. I fear I shall risk death outside rather than melt in that dark furnace. The hills are so honeycombed with caves that the streets look like avenues in a cemetery."

When well-to-do women fled their houses, they were often forced to share quarters with poorer families who resented their presence. The refugees aggravated the situation by expressing contempt for the people with whom they sheltered. Mary Chesnut, who came from an elite South Carolina family, thought that her North Carolina hostess seemed "ladylike and kind ... but she does not brush her teeth—the first evidence of civilization—and lives amidst dirt in a way that would shame the poorest overseer's wife." Such remarks naturally gave offense at the very time when refugees most needed the sympathy and support of strangers.

Growing despair

As the war went on and Union forces moved further into Confederate territory, some poorer Southerners began to despair. Wives began writing to their husbands on the front lines begging them to come home. Other desperate women wrote to officials about their plight, begging for help so that they might remain devoted to the

LETTER FROM HOME

"My Dear Edward,

"I have always been proud of you, and since our connection with the Confederate Army, I have been prouder of you than ever before. I would not have you do anything wrong for the world, but before God, Edward, unless you come home, we must die. Last night I was aroused by little Eddie crying. I called and said, what is the matter, Eddie? And he said, O mamma! I am so hungry. And Lucy, Edward, your darling Lucy, she never complains but she is getting thinner and thinner every day. And before God, Edward, unless you come home, we must die.

   Your Mary"

Letter presented as mitigating evidence in the court martial of a Confederate soldier, Edward Cooper, for desertion.

cause. By the final months of the war thousands of soldiers had deserted, and officials were simply unable to cope with the stream of petitions and requests that covered their desks.

There are few records of how poor Southerners reacted to the end of the war. It seems reasonable to assume, however, that many of them breathed a sigh of relief and turned their attention to their homes and farms. The planter class was much more vocal, expressing its grief and anger at Confederate defeat. As hope died, bitterness grew in its place. The legend of a Lost Cause developed during the Reconstruction era as the defeated Confederates struggled to rebuild their lives in the devastated Southern states.

A Harper's Weekly illustration showing the Confederate evacuation of Brownsville, Texas, in 1864. Brownsville was the "back door to the Confederacy," from where goods were traded across the border with Mexico.

Home front, Union

Civilian life in the Union was not as deeply affected by the war as in the Confederacy. The war barely touched Union soil, the larger population was not hit so hard by the draft, and the people did not go short of food as in the South.

In the autumn of 1862 a Union chaplain on leave in his native Pennsylvania was startled by the prosperity he found at home. Having grown used to war-ravaged Virginia, he wrote, "What a marvel is here! … A nation, from internal resources alone, carrying on for over 18 months the most gigantic war of modern times, ever increasing in its magnitude, yet all the while growing richer and more prosperous!" While this glowing assessment overlooked the many wartime stresses with which Northerners had to contend, it nevertheless captured a basic truth of the conflict. The Union home front, partly from its economic strength and partly from able management, fared remarkably well compared to its Confederate counterpart.

Students at the Academy of Fine Arts in Philadelphia making a flag for the institution during the war. The voluntary activities of Union civilians helped keep up morale.

The people of the Union

To some degree the resilience of the Union home front was to be expected, given the North's advantages in population and resources. In 1860 the North (including the border states) had a population of 21.6 million whites, 248,000 free blacks, plus 430,000 slaves in the border states. In contrast there were only 5.4 million whites in the South, 3.5 million slaves, and 133,000 free blacks. The Northern population was also employed in a wider variety of occupations than in the agricultural South, and the North had a much larger manufacturing and industrial base.

Despite such advantages, if enough Northern men had not stepped forward to join the Union army, if the Northern civilian population had refused to support the war effort, or if Northern leaders had not found ways to mobilize and sustain the economy, the Union would not have been able to win the war. None of these things happened automatically. President Abraham Lincoln's administration could call for

troops, but the federal government was not large enough or strong enough to enforce that call if it was resisted. The support and cooperation of the state governments and local communities was crucial in keeping morale high and encouraging enlistment. By and large, the federal government simply assigned each state a quota of troops and then waited for the states to generate the needed soldiers. Local political, business, and community leaders joined forces to handle the actual work of recruitment.

Initial enthusiasm to volunteer in the Union was high, and state governors asked the federal government to enlarge their quotas. During the war the Union raised more than two million men, including more than 180,000 African Americans. Even though enthusiasm to enlist did not remain as high as in the first months of the war, most Union recruits were volunteers. Congress created a draft in March 1863, but it was only applied in areas that failed to meet their quotas and accounted for only 6 percent of troops.

Those men and women who remained at home had an important role in supporting the war effort by keeping the economy buoyant. Although many men went into the army, many also remained at home to manage the farms or work in industries. They were joined by an increasing number of women in the workforce. For the most part, women served as unskilled laborers, but the war years allowed them to enter certain kinds of employment from which they had previously been barred. Until the Civil War it was almost unheard of in the United States for women to work as government clerks or as nurses, but the acute need for people to perform these functions overcame prewar prejudices.

Strikes and riots

Although the Union's economy did well overall, prices increased more steeply than wages during the war period, and laborers felt the pinch of wartime inflation. Many workers tried to negotiate for higher pay, but with little success. Some went on strike, but the strikes rarely succeeded and on a few occasions were even suppressed by the army. Once the draft was instituted in March 1863—nearly a year after the same step had been taken by the Confederacy—it became another source of discontent on the home front. To the draftees it seemed as if they were being systematically taken advantage of by wealthier Americans who could avoid the draft for a fee of $300. In several places resentment against the draft turned into violence. A number of provost officers lost their lives while attempting to enforce the draft. The worst incident occurred in New York City in July 1863, when

African Americans build barricades to protect the railroad at Alexandria, Virginia, against Confederate attack in 1861. Union troops occupied the town early in the war since it lay across the Potomac River from Washington. The Union made a great effort to make the capital virtually impregnable.

BURNING A NEW YORK ORPHANAGE

Anna Dickinson, an antislavery and women's rights campaigner, describes the burning of an African American orphanage during the New York draft riot of July 1863:

"Late in the afternoon a crowd which could have numbered not less than ten thousand, the majority of whom were ragged, frowsy, drunken women, gathered about the Orphan Asylum for Colored Children—a large and beautiful building and one of the most admirable and noble charities of the city. When it became evident ... that danger, if not destruction, was meditated to the harmless and inoffensive inmates, a flag of truce appeared, and an appeal was made on their behalf ... to every sentiment of humanity which these beings might possess—a vain appeal! Whatever human feeling had ever, if ever, filled these souls was utterly drowned and washed away in the tide of rapine and blood in which they had been steeping themselves. The few [police] officers who stood guard over the doors ... were beaten down ... while the vast crowd rushed in. ... The little ones, many of them assailed and beaten—all, orphans and caretakers, exposed to every indignity and every danger [were] driven on to the street, [and] the building was fired."

angry mobs ransacked draft offices and slaughtered dozens of free blacks (see box), whom they blamed for the war and for conscription. At least 105 people died in the riot.

Politics and patriotism

The draft riot was an extreme manifestation of the opposition felt by many in the Union to the policies of the Lincoln administration. That opposition found political expression in the Democratic Party, once the nation's largest political party and still a powerful minority. The Democrats were divided in their views on the war—most favored a war to preserve the Union, while a significant number preferred a negotiated peace—but they were united in their opposition to emancipation, conscription, and other measures that they considered violations of the U.S.

Union troops who had fought at Gettysburg fire a volley to put down the New York draft riot of July 1863. The riot was the bloodiest civilian disturbance in American history.

A volunteer refreshment saloon for Union troops passing through the railroad station in Philadelphia, Pennsylvania. This lithograph of 1861 commemorates the patriotic work of the citizens of Philadelphia.

Constitution and the philosophy of limited government. To make their views more widely known, Democrats created the Society for the Diffusion of Political Knowledge, an organization to publish pamphlets critical of the Lincoln administration. The Republicans responded with two organizations of their own—the Loyal Publication Society and the Union League—which published nearly 5 million pro-administration pamphlets.

Benevolent societies

An important contribution to the war effort was made by patriotic civilians who banded themselves into voluntary organizations. Soldiers' Aid Associations raised funds, collected supplies, and donated facilities. The U.S. Sanitary Commission, created in 1861, was formed in response to concern about

the health and medical care of Union soldiers. The commission became a highly effective force to promote better hygiene and medical care for troops in the field. It employed paid agents to inspect Northern camps and assigned doctors and ambulances to accompany the armies on active campaign. Huge numbers of people in the Union supported the Sanitary Commission and similar organizations with both money and volunteer assistance. Sanitary fairs in several large Northern cities raised millions of dollars to help their efforts (see box opposite).

Life in the border states

In the Union border states civilian life was deeply affected by the war. Kentucky tried to remain neutral in the conflict but suffered invasion by both Confederate and Union troops. In this fiercely divided state families were split by their loyalty to either side perhaps more than in any other state. In Maryland the Union government came down hard on the supporters of secession. Parts of the state were under occupation, state elections were manipulated, and civilians imprisoned without trial. The border state of Missouri suffered 1,162 battles and skirmishes (a total exceeded only in Virginia and Tennessee), and pro-Union and pro-Confederate guerrilla bands terrorized civilians.

War and society

The impact of the war on civilian life lasted beyond 1865. The increase in the power of the federal government continued into the period of Reconstruction (1865–1877). Women remained in the workforce. Their involvement in war-related volunteer efforts may have enhanced their status in society, although women did not

secure the vote until 50 years later. The service of African Americans in the Union army altered their place in Northern society after the war, although equality remained far in the future.

CIVILIAN FUND-RAISING

Many Northern cities held sanitary fairs to raise funds to buy medical supplies for wounded soldiers and other types of relief. The first such event was held in Chicago on October 27, 1863. The organizers—Mary Livermore and Jane Hoge of the U.S. Sanitary Commission—encouraged people to donate items of interest that they could sell to raise funds. The Chicago fair ran for two weeks and drew 5,000 visitors. The entrance price was 75 cents, and the items on sale included artwork, musical instruments, toys, and clothes. President Lincoln donated the original draft of the Emancipation Proclamation, which was the fair's main attraction and sold at auction for $3,000. The Chicago fair raised $100,000, and following its success, other major cities held fairs. The largest sanitary fair was held in New York in April 1864. Visitors could buy trinkets made by Confederate prisoners of war or even bid for a tame bear or a shipload of coal.

See also

- Democratic Party
- Draft riots
- Economy of the North
- Governors, Union
- Home front, Confederate
- Inflation
- Money and banking
- Politics, Union
- Propaganda
- Recruitment
- Taxation
- Women and the war effort

Five views of the various activities of the women of the U.S. Sanitary Commission, including caring for the wounded, and raising funds for the Union soldiers' welfare.

Hood, John Bell

John Bell Hood (1831–1879) rose quickly through the ranks of the Confederate army. He was an effective, aggressive division commander but proved disastrous in command of the Army of Tennessee, which he led to near-destruction.

John Bell Hood had a poor discipline record at West Point. In his senior year he got 196 demerits and was four short of expulsion halfway through the year.

Hood was born in Kentucky on June 1, 1831. He graduated from the U.S. Military Academy at West Point in 1853. Following U.S. Army service as a cavalry officer in California and Texas, he resigned his lieutenancy in April 1861 and enlisted in the Confederate army. After a number of rapid promotions early in the war Hood attained his brigadier general's star on March 6, 1862, and took command of the renowned Texas Brigade.

Hood's Texans made a bold charge at the Battle of Gaines' Mill on June 27, 1862, which earned the Army of Northern Virginia its first victory. This performance confirmed Hood's reputation as a hard fighter. The Texas Brigade made another successful attack at the Battle of Antietam (Sharpsburg) on September 17, which saved the Confederate left flank. Hood was promoted to major general the following month and given command of a division under James Longstreet.

Division command

Hood continued to distinguish himself in the field. His division played a key part in Longstreet's assault on the second day of the Battle of Gettysburg in July 1863, where Hood was badly wounded in the left arm. At the Battle of Chickamauga on September 20, 1863, Hood suffered a second severe wound and had to have his right leg amputated. He returned to the field in February 1864 as a corps commander in the Army of Tennessee led by General Joseph E. Johnston.

During the campaign to defend Atlanta the overcautious Johnston was removed from command, and Hood was chosen to replace him. Hood launched four major offensives to break the Union siege of Atlanta, but they failed. Hood's aggressive command style also caused grievous casualties in his army. After Atlanta fell in September, Hood retreated north into rural Georgia, where his troops worked to disrupt Union supply lines. In November he invaded Tennessee, hoping to recapture portions of the state. Instead, he destroyed what was left of his army in disastrous battles at Franklin and Nashville. Hood was relieved of command at his own request. After the war Hood lived in New Orleans, where he died from yellow fever in 1879.

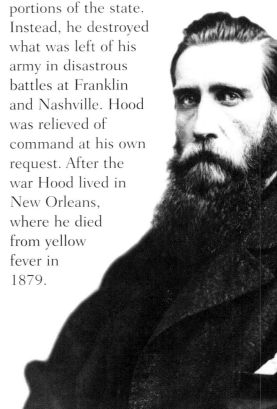

Hooker, Joseph

Joseph Hooker (1814–1879) was a Union general who rose to command the Army of the Potomac in late 1862. Shortly after a crushing Union defeat at the Battle of Chancellorsville in May 1863 Hooker asked to be relieved of his command.

Born in Hadley, Massachusetts, on November 12, 1814, Joseph Hooker graduated from the U.S. Military Academy at West Point in 1837. He fought courageously in the Mexican War (1846–1848) and reached the rank of lieutenant colonel. In 1853 Hooker resigned from the army to run a farm in California.

When the Civil War broke out in 1861, Hooker returned east and took over as brigadier general of volunteers, leading troops in the Peninsular Campaign (April 4–July 1, 1862) against Richmond. He showed great bravery in the Battle of Williamsburg on May 5, 1862, and was promoted to major general of volunteers from this date. When he appeared in a report of the battle as "Fighting Joe," the name stuck, although Hooker himself never liked his nickname. Hooker again showed courage at Second Bull Run (Manassas) in August 1862. He commanded I Corps in the Army of the Potomac at Antietam in September 1862 and was wounded in the foot.

Despite Hooker's prowess in battle, his private life was less controlled. He drank heavily and could be disagreeable and critical of his superiors.

Commanding the Army of the Potomac

In December 1862 President Lincoln promoted Hooker to command of the Army of the Potomac following the army's defeat at Fredericksburg under General Ambrose E. Burnside. In the letter of promotion Lincoln praised Hooker's fighting abilities but also criticized his outspoken opinions—in particular Hooker's idea that the country should be ruled by a military dictator after the war.

At the Battle of Chancellorsville in May 1863 Hooker proved badly indecisive. He was outgeneraled by Robert E. Lee and his Confederate Army of Northern Virginia, who defeated the Union forces despite being outnumbered two to one. Hooker stayed in command for a short while but resigned on June 28 when he was refused reinforcements. He was replaced by General George G. Meade.

Hooker went on to serve ably in the Battle of Lookout Mountain, Tennessee, in November and under William T. Sherman in Georgia. After the war Hooker was passed over for army promotion. He retired following a stroke in 1868 and died in 1879.

On taking command of the Army of the Potomac in December 1862, Joseph Hooker boasted that he would "whip Bobby Lee."

See also

- Antietam (Sharpsburg), Battle of
- Burnside, Ambrose B.
- Chancellorsville, Battle of
- Peninsular Campaign
- Potomac, Army of the

Horses

Civil War armies used horses in their hundreds of thousands. Before the introduction of motorized transportation in the 20th century armies depended on horses for supplies, swift movement in battle, and to maneuver artillery.

Horses had many roles during the Civil War. Cavalrymen charged and fought on horseback, scouts rode on ahead to observe the enemy, and officers in all branches of army service were mounted as a symbol of their rank. Artillery batteries used teams of horses to pull guns and carry ammunition, and the armies relied on horses to help transport supplies.

Transporting supplies

The bulk of army supplies—rations, arms, and equipment—were hauled by railroad and riverboat to collection depots. From there the supplies were transported in wagons pulled by teams of horses or mules to the battle fronts. On campaign the wagon train followed behind the troops. The supply trains could be huge. During Union General

Ulysses S. Grant's invasion of Virginia in 1864 the Army of the Potomac had a wagon train over 5 miles (8km) long, drawn by 500 horses. The task of maintaining an army relied on the regular supply of horses.

Confederate horses

Throughout the war the Confederate army relied on its soldiers, especially its cavalrymen, to provide their own mounts from home. There was no official organization in the Confederacy to keep its army

A blacksmith's forge used by the Union Army of the Potomac during the Siege of Petersburg in Virginia (June 1864–April 1865).

supplied with mounts. The system was adequate for a short war; but as the fighting dragged on, horses in the South were in short supply. By July 1864 General Robert E. Lee was so worried about the lack of cavalry horses that he wrote to President Jefferson Davis suggesting that horses for his army could be purchased in Texas, after which they would cross the Mississippi River by swimming and then be driven the 1,200 miles (1,920km) to Virginia. Lee realized that the journey would be long and arduous but urged Davis to consider the plan: "Even if only a few can be obtained in this way it would be of great assistance."

Union horses

During the early years of war the Union government did not give much thought to the future supply of horses. It was not until July 1863 that it established the Cavalry Bureau to buy and distribute horses to the army. The biggest Union horse depot, at Giesboro near Washington, D.C., covered 600 acres and had stockyards, stables, and forage warehouses to keep 30,000 animals. By 1865 the Union government had spent $124 million supplying its army with mounts.

On campaign even this well-organized system occasionally failed. As Union armies invaded the Southern states, they were tempted simply to take the horses they needed. In late 1864, as Confederates under General John B. Hood were advancing on Nashville, Tennessee, the Union cavalry commander James Wilson found his men short of mounts. He wasted no time in solving his problem. "Within seven days 7,000 horses were obtained in middle and western Kentucky," he

later wrote. "All street-car and livery stable horses, and private carriage and saddle-horses were seized.... A clean sweep was made of every animal that could carry a cavalryman."

Robert E. Lee's sorrel mare, Lucy Long, was stolen near the end of the war. She was found in eastern Virginia after the surrender and returned to Lee.

Medical care

The average life expectancy of horses in Civil War service was just six months. Cavalry mounts were killed or wounded by enemy fire, transport animals died from overwork, and many horses died from disease, exposure, and poor forage in the winter. By fall 1862 the loss of horses to the Confederate Army of Northern Virginia forced it to open a horse hospital at Culpeper Court House, Virginia. By July 1863 Lee's army included more than 6,000 recuperating horses. In the following month the Union army began appointing a veterinary surgeon for every cavalry regiment. Such efforts did not prevent the total deaths of horses and mules in the two armies climbing to an estimated 1.5 million by the end of the war.

Union soldiers burying their dead comrades and burning the dead horses following the Battle of Fair Oaks (Seven Pines) on June 3, 1862, sketched by Alfred Waud.

See also

- Artillery
- Cavalry
- Confederate army
- Hood, John Bell
- Supplies
- Transportation
- Union army

Houses and furniture

The style of houses and furnishings popular during the Civil War era was known as "Victorian" for Queen Victoria, who ruled Great Britain between 1837 and 1901. The style was very ornate, and dark furniture and rich colors were fashionable.

In the 1860s fashionable houses were large, gabled dwellings with porches and "gingerbread" trim that were painted in shades of yellow, red, and brown. Inside, rooms shone with rich colors—deep carmine, gilt, and sky blue—and were filled with a clutter of parlor suites, writing bureaus, coatracks, tables, and chairs. Later generations considered all things Victorian ugly and overcrowded. At the time of the Civil War, however, intricate and rich interiors were very popular.

Victorian values

The term "Victorian" refers generally to the culture of English-speaking peoples on both sides of the Atlantic Ocean in the 19th century. At that time Britain and the United States were experiencing rapid industrialization, which led to increasing numbers of Americans becoming part of the middle class. Along with owners of businesses, doctors, lawyers, teachers, and ministers, this group expanded to include new salaried employees who worked as managers, technicians, clerks, and engineers. No longer working on family farms, these people instead worked in towns and cities. Long working hours earned their families a modest status and enough money to live in some style and comfort, and they wanted houses and furnishings to match their new rank.

A prosperous city dweller in the North might choose to build a two-story masonry house. A less well-off clerk in the city might move his family to the new suburbs away from the noise, dirt, and danger of the city, where he could afford to pay for the construction of a new home. A poor family living in the

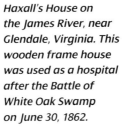

Haxall's House on the James River, near Glendale, Virginia. This wooden frame house was used as a hospital after the Battle of White Oak Swamp on June 30, 1862.

same growing city could only afford to rent a small apartment in a tenement building shared with other lodgers. In rural areas of the North a family might construct a farmhouse or occupy one that had been built much earlier.

In the Southern states a prosperous merchant in the commercial port of New Orleans might live in a fashionable two-story brick dwelling. In other Southern centers of commerce, such as Savannah, Charleston, and Richmond, there were many stylish and up-to-date houses. However, the overwhelmingly rural areas of the South had an altogether different architecture. A nonslaveholding farmer might live in a simple wooden frame house. It would have little in common with either the slave huts or the elegant plantation home of a wealthy landowner nearby.

In all but the most expensive houses people tended to use building materials that were close at hand and in ready supply. In the forested areas of the Southeast and Northeast people built wooden frame houses and log cabins with the plentiful supplies of wood. In the Southwest, where the arid climate meant there was little vegetation, people built houses of adobe bricks. Adobe was made from clay moistened with water and lime, and then baked by the sun into large bricks.

Architectural styles

Very wealthy people were able to build their homes in a specific style—those popular at the time were the Gothic Revival and Italianate styles. Gothic Revival was the earliest Victorian style. It was inspired by European medieval architecture, especially castles and churches, and so had features such as pointed arches and battlements.

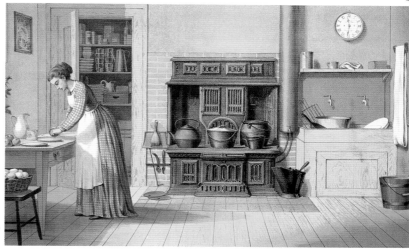

The Italianate style was influenced by Italian country villas. A distinctive feature of this style was the use of brackets—L-shaped pieces of carved wood up under the eaves. Italianate houses had low-pitched or flat roofs; and unlike earlier houses, which were usually painted white, they were often painted in blues, greens, and yellows.

Few houses in the South were built at this time in these new styles, however. The fine homes of the prewar South tended to continue the earlier Greek Revival style. This style was inspired by the buildings of ancient Greece and had come to the United States from Britain. Greek Revival houses had a symmetrical floor plan with a wide central hall that allowed air to circulate freely during the warmer months. They were usually white, with tall windows that often reached the floor. The front of Greek Revival buildings often resembled the entrance to a Greek temple with tall pillars.

Immediately after the Civil War, when the Gothic Revival and Italianate styles became increasingly popular, there was little money in the South to spend on new furniture and houses. Within a decade or so, however, the

An 1873 illustration of a kitchen in Boston, Massachusetts. In the center is the kitchen range, which was found in most new homes of the time, and was used for cooking and heating water.

A tenement building on Mulberry Street on the Lower East Side, Manhattan, illustrated in Harper's Weekly, September 13, 1873. As the population of New York grew, tenements became notorious for providing overcrowded and unhealthy living conditions.

Inside the home

The outside appearance of a house was a good indication of a family's status and wealth. Likewise, the look of the rooms inside conveyed a message to those who visited the home. The interior of a house was expected to provide a very different space from the materialistic outside world of work. The home was to serve as a special place of spiritual renewal in which family members would want to gather. The interior decoration therefore took on a special meaning. Magazines and books gave advice on matters such as colors, furniture, lighting, and wallpapers.

fashionable architectural styles of the Victorian era began to be seen in the Southern states.

House designs

Not all houses were built in a particular style. Much American architecture at this time was "vernacular," which means commonplace. In 19th-century America the profession of architecture was only just getting started. A few architects did publish plan books, however, which included line drawings of exteriors and measured floor plans. Builders copied these published designs for wealthy clients. Soon afterward Americans had opportunities to buy plans for their homes from magazines and mail-order catalogues.

THE HATRACK

Ellen Bowie Holland in her memoir of her girlhood in North Texas, remembered one piece of furniture in particular:

"A hatrack was a very articulate piece of furniture. From the conglomeration hanging on it, at a glance, you could tell if Uncle Harry, Cousin Frank, or the Misses McGruders were being entertained—and it was exciting to see a strange flowered hat, a city derby, or a feather boa. Our hatrack was the biggest, ugliest piece of furniture made since they divided all Gaul into three parts. But we didn't know it. It was simply accepted as a necessity. It was of oak and around a mirror bristled six fancy double brass prongs. The lower part was an armed seat and the top of the seat was hinged like a chest. It opened and when we came home we dumped our extra fribbles into it. Whenever anything was lost someone would say, 'Have you looked in the hatrack?'"

In the Victorian era men presided over the house, while women were responsible for creating interior spaces that provided a comfortable living space and displayed how cultured the family was. They accomplished this by decorating the home with handiwork such as embroidery or painted china.

The furniture that filled homes of the Civil War era may have been handed down through the family, bought from local cabinetmakers, or imported from manufacturers in the big cities. New furniture often took inspiration from old historical styles, such as Gothic, Elizabethan, Rococo, and Louis XVI.

Heating and plumbing

Builders took the climate into consideration when building houses, since there was no way to regulate the temperature by air-conditioning or central heating. Electricity was not available until much later in the century. Rooms were lighted by candles or kerosene lamps. A few houses had gas lighting, especially in cities where piped gas was just being introduced. Very few homes had running water. The lack of indoor plumbing meant that all water had to be drawn by hand, and chamber pots and outhouses had to be used instead of flush toilets.

Polite behavior

Before the Victorian period rooms usually served several purposes—socializing, sleeping, and even eating. Now rooms became specialized. A hall, formal parlor, family parlor, dining room, library, bedroom—all served specific functions and required certain activities and behavior. Knowing how to behave appropriately in these settings and follow the social rules correctly defined a person's place in society and showed whether or not he or she was a refined person. In a rapidly changing society these complex rules of behavior helped establish the social order.

See also

- Daily life
- Food
- Home front, Confederate
- Home front, Union
- Plantation life
- Urban life

Oak Alley Plantation, Vacherie, Louisiana, Built in 1839 by a New Orleans sugar planter, it is an example of the classical Greek Revival style of plantation house built before the Civil War.

Illinois

The pride that the people of Illinois continue to take in their state's role in the Civil War and their most famous resident is demonstrated by the words placed on every Illinois automobile license plate: "Land of Lincoln."

Illinois played a vital role in the events that led up to the Civil War and in the conduct of the war. Since its southern border reached farther south than Richmond, Virginia, Illinois had a large population that had migrated from the slave states. The north of the state was settled by people from New England and New York. The mixture made Illinois a political battleground leading up to the Civil War.

Douglas and Lincoln

In 1858 the Senate race between Republican Abraham Lincoln and Democrat Stephen A. Douglas became a national forum for the debate between proslavery and antislavery advocates, mainly concerning the controversial issue of the expansion of slavery into the territories. The seven Lincoln–Douglas debates took place at places around Illinois.

Douglas won the election as senator, but two years later he once more found himself opposed by Lincoln, this time for the U.S. presidency. Douglas was at that time the most famous Democratic politician in the nation. Lincoln, in contrast, was known only through his debates with Douglas. It was largely because the Republican Convention was held in Chicago, Illinois, that Lincoln's name, after three ballots, emerged as the unexpected candidate for the White House. After Lincoln defeated Douglas for the presidency, Douglas helped rally Northern Democrats to help Lincoln fight the secession of the Southern states.

Cost to the state

Illinois made a major contribution to the winning of the Civil War. Nearly 260,000 men from the state served in the Union army. Illinois troops played a major role in most of the battles fought in the western theater of operations, from the campaign for Fort Donelson in 1862 to Sherman's infamous March to the Sea in 1864. At Shiloh, for example, 28 of the 65 Union regiments engaged

Abraham Lincoln's house in Springfield, Illinois. He bought it in 1844 for $1,200, and it was his home for 17 years until he moved to Washington, D.C., to take up his duties as U.S. president.

DU PAGE COUNTY CENTENNIAL

LINCOLN · DOUGLAS

DEBATE

AUGUST · 27TH
WEST CHICAGO

which organized soldier relief. Mary Livermore of Chicago organized the first of a series of Sanitary Fairs—temporary shopping malls with food courts, exhibits, and theaters where donated goods were sold. She raised hundreds of thousands of dollars for soldier relief and served to rally civilian support for the war effort.

Chicago

Chicago, the state's great metropolis on the shores of Lake Michigan, was a tremendous hub of production during the Civil War. The task of supplying the Union army with the agricultural bounty of the Midwest helped develop the city into a transportation and industrial center.

During the war Chicago became the nation's meatpacking capital and a leading producer of steel railroad track and rolling stock. The number of factories in the city tripled during the 1860s. In stark contrast to the prosperity of the city were the wretched conditions found at the Camp Douglas prisoner-of-war camp located just to its south. During the course of the war more than 4,400 Confederate prisoners died at the camp.

Left: A poster advertising one of the seven Lincoln–Douglas debates during the Illinois senatorial campaign in 1854. The main topic was the extension of slavery into the territories.

in combat were from Illinois. So great were Illinois's losses in the battle that Governor Richard Yates ordered that several steamboats be converted into floating hospitals to remove the thousands of suffering men from the battlefield. By the end of the war the number of Illinois troops who had lost their lives was nearly 35,000.

Illinois women

Mary Ann Bickerdyke, a widow from central Illinois, followed Sherman's army, tending their wounds. When an army surgeon questioned her on whose authority she was with the army, "Mother" Bickerdyke (as the soldiers called her) replied, "I have received my authority from the Lord God Almighty. Have you a higher authority?"

On the home front Illinois women were active in the growth and success of the Northwest Sanitary Commission,

Military leaders

Illinois produced several important Union military leaders during the war. The most famous was Ulysses S. Grant, who was working as a clerk in a shop in Galena, Illinois, when the war broke out. He was appointed colonel of the 21st Illinois Infantry in 1861 and eventually rose to become the general-in-chief of all the Union armies. Two former Illinois politicians, John A. Logan and John A. McClernand, rose to the rank of major general.

Immigrants

A surge in immigration in the decades before the Civil War meant that by 1860 the ethnic composition of the United States was rapidly changing. More than 500,000 foreign-born soldiers fought in the war, overwhelmingly for the Union.

A huge majority of the immigrant populations settled in the free-labor states of the North rather than the Southern slave states, which contributed to the feeling that the two sections were growing ever further apart. Immigration played a major part in the political turmoil and disintegration that led to a party realignment along sectional lines in the late 1850s, and that in turn led directly to secession and war.

Immigration was not a very large feature of life during the first 50 years of American independence. Even in the 1820s, when the number of immigrants began to grow, there were fewer than 130,000 new arrivals (representing just 1 in 100 out of a population of 13 million in 1830). Between 1830 and 1840, however, there was a quadrupling of immigrants to the United States. As had been the case from the Republic's earliest days, the great majority of these immigrants were Protestants, mainly from Britain; and while many of them were farmers, many others were skilled or white-collar workers.

Dramatic change

During the 1840s and 1850s there was a dramatic change in the scale and pattern of immigration. Repeated failure of the potato crop in Ireland and

An 1866 engraving of the first immigrant-processing center in the United States, set up in 1855 on Castle Garden, an island off Manhattan, New York.

THE KNOW-NOTHINGS

The nativist Know-Nothings were a powerful political force in the decade leading up to the Civil War. Their origins lay in a number of secret fraternal orders whose membership was restricted to native-born Protestants. From 1852 these organizations were welded together into a national force with perhaps as many as a million members. The members pledged to vote only for native-born Protestants and to fend off any questions from outsiders about the order by responding, "I know nothing." This led to them being dubbed "Know-Nothings," and the name stuck.

Because of their secrecy and commitment the Know-Nothings were a powerful political influence, and they helped polarize many of the burning issues of the day, including slavery. The Democratic Party was seen as the immigrant's friend, and Irish Catholics in particular overwhelmingly supported it. The Democratic Party was also seen as slavery's friend. Know-Nothings were thus inclined to link slavery with Catholicism as fundamentally foreign to the American way of life. By 1860, however, the Know-Nothings had largely faded from the scene since the new Republican Party seemed to have a more secure grip on the impending crisis over the slavery issue.

An 1854 sheet music cover illustrated with Know-Nothing motifs, including animals and plants native to North America.

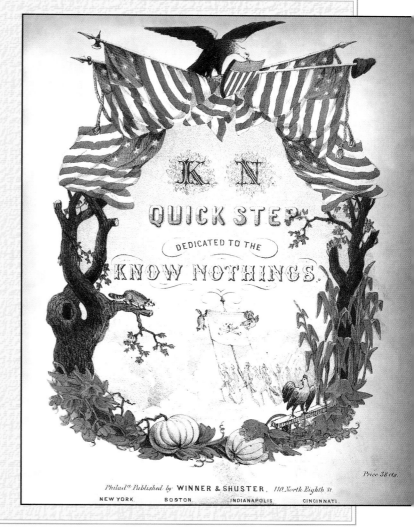

political and economic upheaval in Germany created a huge influx of immigration to the United States from these two countries. Just under 1.5 million arrived in the 1840s and 2.8 million in the 1850s. Since the population was 31 million in 1860, that meant that now nearly 1 in every 10 Americans had arrived in the previous decade. More than 60 percent of these new immigrants were Roman Catholics from Ireland and Germany, and a great many of the Irish in particular were poor, unskilled laborers.

Overwhelmingly this influx was concentrated in the large cities of the Northeast, in New York, Boston, and Philadelphia, where squalid, overcrowded tenements became a feature of urban life. By 1860, 39 percent of the foreign-born population of the United States was Irish and 31 percent German.

Immigration on this scale and of this type did not go unchallenged. There were sporadic anti-Catholic riots in the big cities, and so-called "nativist" political parties emerged that attempted

A drawing by Alfred Waud of St. Patrick's Day sports in the Irish Brigade of the Union Army of the Potomac in 1863. This brigade, commanded by Thomas F. Meagher, was the most famous Irish unit.

to slow down the pace at which immigrants could achieve full citizenship rights. At the height of its influence the nativist political movement contributed to the breakdown of the existing two-party system that preceded the Civil War. In the end it was the antislavery Republican Party that emerged from the ruins of the Whig Party in the 1850s, but in the early years of the decade a powerful new nativist party known as the Know-Nothings was attracting considerable political support (see box on page 25).

Wartime immigration

During the first two years of the war immigration fell sharply, but it picked up again in 1863 because of labor shortages. Many immigrants jumped at the generous bounties offered to join the Union army—of the two million white men who saw service in Union colors about one in four was foreign-born. This gave rise to the Southern charge that the Union was fighting the war with "foreign hirelings." In truth,

however, it was simply a reflection of how much more attractive a prospect it was for immigrants to carve out a new life in the free-labor North rather than the slaveholding South.

Lincoln made an effort to court immigrants in the 1860 election and then rewarded their leaders with army appointments. These men then recruited their countrymen once war broke out. Despite having suffered hostility from native-born Americans in the 1850s, immigrants volunteered for the Union army across the North. Companies of various nationalities were raised, including French, Scandinavian, Italian, German, and Irish units. Several units, such as the Irish Brigade, achieved fame for their bravery. The immigrant volunteers often brought valuable military experience, having seen action in the Crimean War or in the uprisings that had taken place across Europe in 1848.

Six foreign-born soldiers achieved the rank of major general in the Union army. Although the Confederate army had fewer high-ranking officers—partly because it had far fewer foreign-born soldiers—two immigrant soldiers did reach the rank of major general.

Draft riots

In July 1863 riots broke out in New York City in protest at the Conscription Act. It was widely regarded as unfair because it allowed a man to avoid military service for a fee of $300 or if he could hire a substitute. Irish immigrants were prominent in the looting and violence that lasted for four days and nights. By the time the disturbances petered out on July 17, the city had been shattered, and more than a hundred people had been killed.

Impressment

As inflation in the Confederacy soared and money lost value, the government turned to taxing its people in goods and impressing (seizing) whatever it needed to fight the war, including food, animals, clothes, and slaves.

The act that gave the Confederate government the right to impress private property for the maintenance of the army and navy was passed on March 6, 1863. All private property could be impressed by the army for public use, although breeding livestock was exempted in March 1865.

Impressment officers were appointed by state governors to seize cattle, clothing, food, horses, iron, railroads, domestic and industrial property, slaves, and even freedmen. Compensation for the impressed property was set by a price schedule and by two independent parties, one chosen by the impressment officer, the other appointed by the property owner. Impressment of freedmen was like a draft—the laborers were compensated personally with an established minimum wage.

At the beginning of the war the Union government already had the power to impress private property in military emergencies. However, the government seldom took advantage of the right because the Union was not as short of supplies as the Confederacy.

Response to impressment

The Confederate law of March 1863 simply legalized established practice and was an attempt to regulate the behavior of army units. Confederate armies already used impressment in emergencies and paid for the goods later when the owner brought compensation claims. Nevertheless the law was widely unpopular. Many Southern governors complained to the War Department, taking the view that the power of impressment violated state and individual rights. Governor Zebulon B. Vance of North Carolina described impressment, in particular when imposed by an undisciplined cavalry unit, as a "plague worse than all others." In spring 1863 the Confederate government took another unpopular measure to sustain the army, passing a 10 percent "tax in kind" on farm produce. Southerners regarded this as impressment under another name.

Opposition to impressment grew in the last months of the war, when the price schedule was abandoned. Impressment officers needed only to give a "just price" for impressed goods. The "just price" took no account of the rapid inflation of Confederate currency. Many people believed the vagueness of the phrase allowed officers to make personal profit.

An impressment receipt for a 22-year old slave. The power of the Confederate army to impress slaves and other private property for the war effort was bitterly opposed by many Southerners.

See also

- Confederate army
- Confederate government
- Governors, Confederate
- Home front, Confederate
- Inflation
- Supplies
- Taxation

Indiana

Although many Indiana residents had Confederate sympathies, the state remained in the Union. The fifth largest of the Union states, Indiana was one of the main sources of food for the Northern armies throughout the Civil War.

In 1861 Indiana was completely unprepared for war—its militia had been neglected by politicians since the American Revolution, and the state had no trained soldiers. Yet the Hoosiers rallied magnificently. Indiana was one of the first states to respond to President Abraham Lincoln's April 15 call for 75,000 soldiers, quickly meeting its original quota of 7,500 and having to turn away many disappointed men eager to fight for the Union.

Even after early optimism in the North that the Southern states would easily be crushed had given way to realization that the war would be long

Company H of the 44th Indiana Infantry, one of the 129 infantry regiments raised in Indiana during the Civil War.

and harsh, enthusiasm in Indiana remained undimmed. Within a year many Indiana veterans of the Mexican War (1846–1848) and other former servicemen had gone back voluntarily into uniform. By the end of 1862 more than 61,300 Hoosiers had enlisted, nearly twice the number demanded by Lincoln in his second appeal for troops.

Quality leadership

Indiana's outstanding contribution to the Union war effort was due in large measure to the efforts of Oliver P. Morton, its wartime governor. He is widely considered to be one of the most effective state governors of the period. Confronted at the start of his term of office in 1861 by a hostile Democratic majority in the statehouse, Morton took

unilateral action to get his state on a war footing. He was forced to violate Indiana's constitution by borrowing, without authorization, the millions of dollars needed to raise and equip an army. Most of the money was advanced by a single New York bank, and it is a testament to Morton's powers of persuasion that he managed to convince its proprietors to overlook Indiana's previous bad payment record. Morton used the funds to set up training camps, buy war equipment, establish a state arsenal, and provide for hospital care and the welfare of soldiers and their dependents.

Morton is credited with raising as many as 150,000 men for the Union armies with little resort to the draft. He did this because he believed in the Union cause and opposed secession, not because he was unreserved in his support for Lincoln. Indeed, he clashed with the president several times, opposing Lincoln's policies to arrest dissidents, free Southern slaves, and also on the principle of the draft itself.

Indiana troops

By the end of the Civil War Indiana had contributed nearly 208,400 soldiers to the Union cause. The state's military forces included 129 infantry regiments, 13 cavalry regiments, 3 mounted companies, 1 regiment of heavy artillery, and 26 batteries of light artillery. The 19th Indiana Infantry, part of the famous Iron Brigade, suffered the highest percentage of soldiers killed —16 percent, a total of 199 out of 1,246 men.

Indiana regiments were engaged in every major Civil War battle, from the opening attack on Fort Sumter, where Hoosier Jefferson C. Davis served as a

lieutenant, to the final engagement of the conflict at Palmetto Ranch, Texas. The human cost to the state was high: More than 7,200 Hoosiers were killed in action, another 17,800 died of disease, and more than twice that number were injured.

Morgan's Raid

The only significant engagement in Indiana took place in July 1863, when the legendary Confederate cavalry raider John H. Morgan led about 3,000 cavalrymen across the Ohio River into the southern part of the state, where there were Southern sympathizers. Morgan hoped that his invasion would spark an uprising by local Copperheads (Northerners sympathetic to the South), but for reasons that are unclear no such backing ever materialized. Morgan's men clashed with the Indiana home guard on July 9 at the Battle of Corydon, taking most of them captive. For the next five days the Confederate raiders plundered and looted before Union troops converged to drive them into the neighboring state of Ohio.

Confederate prisoners at Camp Morton, near Indianapolis, Indiana, in 1863. Originally a place of rendezvous for volunteers, Camp Morton became a prisoner-of-war camp from 1862, typically holding about 3,500 Confederate soldiers.

See also

- Copperheads
- Governors, Union
- Lincoln, Abraham
- Recruitment
- Union army

Industry in the 1860s

In 1860 the United States was poised to become a great industrial power, but its industry was concentrated in the Northern states. The small industrial base in the South hampered the Confederacy's war effort.

Miner's Foundry in San Francisco. The conical "shot tower" was used to manufacture lead shot. Molten lead was dropped from the top of the tower into a vat of water at the bottom. The lead droplets formed perfect spheres when they cooled on contact with the water.

There were two key divisions between the North and South on the eve of war. The first was Southern slavery; the other was rapid Northern industrialization. The relative industrial backwardness of the South was one of the Confederacy's gravest handicaps and plagued its war effort throughout.

During the prolonged crisis that led to secession, Southern economic subordination to the North was a hotly debated issue. It rankled with proud Southerners to see their region slipping behind the free states. At the same time, it reinforced their belief that the South was a unique society—a stable farming community that protected an attractive way of life for whites. Southerners also argued that industrial workers in the North were no better off than slaves. They pointed to poverty and overcrowding in Northern cities and the inhumanity of working long hours in airless factories for a pittance. Envy of Northern prosperity was combined with contempt for the methods that made progress possible.

The widening gulf

The industrial gulf between the two regions widened in the two decades before the war. In 1840 there were nearly as many miles of railroad in the slave states as free states. By 1860, in relation to its population and size, the North was about twice as well served by rail as the South. Four-fifths of the nation's factories were in the free states, and they accounted for nearly 90 percent of total manufacturing. Cotton textile manufacture in the South, where the bulk of the world's raw cotton was grown, represented only 10 percent of the American total in 1860. The figure for the manufacture of boots and shoes was the same. Northern states manufactured 93 percent of the nation's pig iron (crude iron as it comes out of the blast furnace) and 97 percent of its firearms.

RIBBONS OF STEEL

Railroads were extremely important during the Civil War for both civilian and military purposes. They continued their prewar activities of transporting people and goods while also serving to move large numbers of troops and supplies over great distances. At the outset of war the Confederacy closed the Mississippi River to Union traffic, but the North was able to rely instead on its existing east–west rail systems, which included the Baltimore & Ohio, the Erie, and the Pennsylvania. Railroad building slowed down in the North in the first years of the war, but the existing system was well maintained and then expanded by the capture of railroads in the Confederacy.

A 1860s advertisement for a new type of railroad bridge. The Union expanded its rail network during the Civil War.

The Confederacy lacked the resources to expand or even to maintain its existing railroad network, which by 1865 lay virtually in ruins. Meanwhile, the Union had sufficient manpower and resources to start work on the first transcontinental railroad in 1863 and laid 20 miles (32km) of track eastward from Sacramento, California.

Complacency about the superiority of the Southern way of life was difficult to sustain in the face of such evidence. In 1851 a Southern newspaper editor tried to persuade Southerners to invest in industry and build factories of all varieties by pointing out that Southern slaves wore Northern-made clothes and worked with "Northern hoes, plows, and other implements." He continued to rail against slaveholders who scorned Northern industry but were similarly dependent on Northern products— not only their clothes, carriages, and saddles, but also the books they read, and the pen, paper, and ink they wrote with were manufactured in the North.

In a series of annual conventions that took place until the outbreak of war, progressive Southerners debated ways to shake the region out of its commercial sleepiness. In particular there were calls to set up a Southern shipbuilding industry so that the South could trade with Europe without relying on European and Northern ships. There was also agitation to build a railroad west to the Pacific Coast. Plans were put forward to build factories that would provide the economic strength and diversity to resist the mounting political pressure from the free states. Economic equality with the North would help the South assert its rights.

Urgent need for industry

While industrial activity in the Southern states improved during the 1850s, the war nevertheless exposed its limitations. When the Union naval blockade of the Southern coast began to strangle Southern trade, the Confederacy realized the urgent need to expand its industry at home. The need was so great that the Confederate

The Tredegar Works in Richmond was the only major ironworks in the South in 1860. On the outbreak of war the owner of Tredegar sent a telegram to the Confederate government promising to "make anything you want—work day and night if necessary."

See also

• Economy of the North
• Economy of the South
• Railroads
• Trade
• Urban life

government decided that it could not rely on private enterprise to respond quickly enough. In a break with prewar tradition government departments allocated resources to build factories. Gunpowder mills and ordnance factories were built in major cities such as Atlanta and Richmond. The long-established Tredegar Works honored its pledge to produce enough iron to meet almost all the Confederacy's military and transportation needs. Despite substantial difficulties, Confederate industry did manage to keep the army supplied with guns and ammunition to the end. The industrial advances were not permanent, however, since many new industries were destroyed by the Union armies.

Industry in the Union flourishes

The Union's initial superiority in terms of industrial strength was magnified in the course of the war. This was partly in direct response to the increase in

demand for equipment and supplies, but also because of changes in the labor market brought on by the war. The shortage of labor led to rapid improvements in mechanization in key industries. In the garment industry the introduction of the sewing machine vastly increased the productivity of seamstresses making military uniforms and other clothing. There was also a huge increase in the employment of women, not only in industry but in agriculture as well. With nearly a million Northern farmers under arms neglect of the farms could have resulted in shortages—at it did in the Confederacy. Instead, revolutionary new reapers and harvesters substituted horsepower for human power, and farming women took to them with enthusiasm. Instead of falling, farm productivity rose rapidly in the Union.

The economic productivity of the Union was startling. After a decline in the first year of the war caused by the loss of Southern markets it climbed to unprecedented heights. In 1864 iron production was nearly a third higher than it had ever been for the country as a whole. Coal production increased in similar proportions. Merchant ship-building increased, and the Union navy grew to nearly 700 ships—making it the largest in the world. An armaments industry that in 1861 could not begin to equip the Union armies was more than able to do so by 1865, despite the huge growth in army numbers. Canal and railroad traffic soared as the booming war economy expanded the internal market. The industrial triumph of the Union heralded the success of postwar American industry, which overtook the industry of Great Britain and Germany within a generation of the Civil War.

Infantry tactics

Infantry tactics changed considerably during the course of the Civil War. Changes were brought about by the introduction of new weapons, especially the rifled musket, which had a greater range and accuracy than previous weapons.

The Union and the Confederacy used similar battle tactics during the Civil War since many generals had been taught at the same military schools and had served together in the U.S. Army before the war. Their field officers, who led the men into combat, were mostly volunteers. They had to learn battle maneuvers from books, such as Hardee's *Tactics*, a manual widely read by officers on both sides.

The basic objective of infantry tactics was to be able to maneuver units of troops into a position where they could deploy on the battlefield as quickly and efficiently as possible, so as to bring the maximum amount of musket fire onto the enemy and then to charge with bayonets and drive the enemy from the field. Confederate commander "Stonewall" Jackson's brigade broke the Union attack on Henry Hill using exactly these tactics in the First Battle of Bull Run (Manassas) in July 1861.

Training and drill

To achieve this result, infantry companies were trained to march in column, usually four men across. On an order they could change formation and direction and, without altering pace, deploy into a battle line two ranks deep 16 inches (40cm) apart facing the enemy. They were then ordered to load and fire their muskets. A regiment had to retain its coordination in battle to be effective. Constant training and drill were needed to accomplish this, in addition to strictly following the orders shouted by officers or signaled by bugle calls or drums.

This method of getting large numbers of men into combat was adaptable enough to allow infantry units of any size to deploy for action using the same maneuvers. A regiment could form a line by deploying its companies and a brigade by deploying its regiments.

The battle line itself did not form a solid wall of soldiers. To allow room for units to maneuver, tactical manuals recommended a 20-yard (18.5m) gap between regiments and a 25-yard (23m)

A bayonet charge of Union troops at the Battle of Fair Oaks (Seven Pines), Virginia, in June 1862. This method of attack became obsolete as the introduction of more accurate weapons made a frontal assault without any cover an act of suicide.

gap between brigades. Regiments could also hold companies behind the line in reserve or advance companies forward in a skirmish line up to 500 yards (450m) ahead of the main formation.

Skirmishers operated in "open order," each man spaced a few yards from next, taking advantage of available cover to keep the enemy line under fire. They also maintained contact with the enemy and gave warning if they began to move forward for an attack.

Method of attack

The most common method of attack was to advance lines of regiments or brigades one after the other in waves about 25 yards (23m) apart. Often the first wave was used as cover for the rest by advancing it up to 300 yards (275m) in front so as to take all the enemy fire: The first wave kept the succeeding units relatively safe from enemy bullets. The speed of the attack depended on the distance to be covered. There was

no point in exhausting the men in the charge so that they were out of breath when they reached the enemy. Instead, an attack was made at regulation quick time, a march of 110 steps per minute, which covered about 86 yards (78m). In theory, lines struck the enemy positions in straight disciplined ranks, but in practice this was rarely accomplished. As a Southern officer wrote, "Whoever saw a Confederate line advancing that was not crooked as a ram's horn [with] each ragged rebel yelling on his own hook and aligning on himself?"

New tactics

Tactics changed as the war went on, however. The tactics laid down in the manuals had been perfected in Europe in the Napoleonic Wars of the early 1800s. The U.S. Army used them successfully during the Mexican War (1846–1848), but they were out of date by 1861. The main reason for this was that the tactics were developed at a

The 96th Pennsylvania Infantry drilling at Camp Northumberland in 1861. Constant drilling was essential to deploy troops successfully on the battlefield.

time when the infantryman's weapon was the smoothbore flintlock musket, which was inaccurate and had an effective range of only 60 yards (55m). In the 1860s the introduction of rifled muskets dramatically changed how battles were fought. The new rifled muskets could kill at 500 yards (450m). Such weapons made the bayonet charge very dangerous and standing in line without cover a few hundred yards from the enemy an act of suicide.

Importance of using cover

Although charging in ranks in the face of enemy fire was dangerous, that did not stop army commanders throughout the war from holding onto the belief that such attacks could win battles. The Civil War was marked by a series of bloody and futile frontal assaults, such as the Union charges on Marye's Heights during the Battle of Fredericksburg in December 1862. By 1864 soldiers were changing the way they were fighting as a result of bitter experience. Infantry attacks were now made in short rushes, with soldiers giving each other covering fire as they ran from one place of safety to another.

Defensive trenches

In defense, getting out of the way of enemy fire became the first priority, and entrenchments were widely dug. Union General William T. Sherman wrote of his men in the last year of war: "Troops halting for the night or for battle, faced the enemy; moved forward to ground with a good outlook to the front; stacked arms; gathered logs, fence-rails; anything that would stop a bullet; piled these in front, and digging a ditch behind threw the dirt forward, and made a parapet which covered their persons as perfectly as a granite wall."

As another Union general, Jacob D. Cox, explained after the war, "One rifle in the trench was worth five in front of it." These were to become the new tactics that would dominate infantry warfare in the next 50 years.

Confederate troops use the huge boulders on Culp's Hill as cover during the Battle of Gettysburg, July 1863. As new, more effective weapons became widely used, soldiers fought from behind some form of cover wherever possible.

See also

- Artillery
- Cavalry
- Confederate army
- Fredericksburg, Battle of
- Training
- Union army
- Weapons and firearms

Inflation

Both the Union and the Confederacy printed paper money to meet the cost of the war. These paper notes suffered from inflation; in other words, they lost real value over time. In the Confederacy inflation reached catastrophic heights.

The auction of a gold piece at Danville, Virginia, in February 1864. The Confederate currency suffered such severe inflation that by 1865 it took $90 in paper notes to buy one prewar gold dollar.

While the Union used an effective combination of methods to finance the war, the Confederacy relied too heavily on simply printing paper notes in order to pay its bills. Confederate notes began to lose value as soon as they were printed. This loss of value, termed inflation, reached a ruinous 9,000 percent, which meant that $1 was worth little more than a prewar cent. By contrast, total inflation in the Union was 80 percent.

Both sides were reluctant to impose heavy taxes to finance the war since taxes were unpopular. They borrowed money, but that was not enough. Each government, therefore, turned to the printing presses. In February 1862 the U.S. Congress authorized the issue of paper currency that was not backed by gold or silver, the principle on which all monetary systems traditionally rested. The Union government compelled acceptance of these notes, which made them legal tender, a step the Confederates did not take. The Union paper dollars were quickly nicknamed greenbacks. By the end of the war $450 million in greenbacks was in circulation. Their value in relation to gold held up well for wartime, and the notes were retained after 1865.

Confederate inflation

The Confederacy took similar measures but with disastrous consequences. Secretary of the Treasury Christopher G. Memminger began by issuing $20 million in paper money in May 1861. In total, Southern printing presses churned out $1.5 billion. The value of the notes relied on public confidence that the Confederacy would win the war and ultimately prosper. When the Confederate army's fortunes dipped, so did the value of the currency. By late 1863 $1 was worth one-seventh of what it had been before the war. By the end of the war Southerners viewed their own currency as virtually worthless. The diarist Mary Chesnut wrote of her relief when a shop would accept Confederate notes at all: "I never stop to bargain. I give them $20 or $50 cheerfully for anything—either sum."

Intellectuals

As with material resources, educational and intellectual resources were heavily skewed in favor of the free-labor Northern states. The leading intellectuals of the United States at the time were almost exclusively from New England.

New England had a distinguished educational tradition —it led the world in literacy at the time—and that was reflected in the attainments of America's great 19th-century thinkers and writers. This was the "flowering of New England" that represented the birth of original American intellectual activity, independent from European models. It included Ralph Waldo Emerson of Boston and his disciple Henry David Thoreau of Concord, the novelist Nathaniel Hawthorne of Salem, and his friend the poet Henry Wadsworth Longfellow of Maine. These outstanding figures were representative of the finest American thinkers of the day. All of them took a keen interest in the rift between the North and South that finally erupted into war.

Antislavery supporters
The New England intellectuals had no sympathy with slavery; most supported abolition to a greater or lesser extent. For example, when John Brown went to the gallows after his attack at Harpers Ferry in 1859, Thoreau called him "a crucified hero." Longfellow wrote that Brown's execution marked a "new Revolution."

Hawthorne and Emerson were fervent admirers of President Abraham Lincoln, and greeted his Emancipation Proclamation of 1862 with enthusiasm.

The war affected the intellectual mind just as it did any other that reflected on its brutalities and cruel necessities. Emerson, for example, was world famous for his views on individualism and the sacred quality of liberty. Yet in 1862 he was able to write that in such a crisis as the nation found itself, he would be prepared to grant government "the absolute powers of a dictator." Emerson may have been exaggerating to make his point, which was that private good had to be weighed against public duty and, if necessary, subordinated to it. Emerson was not alone in coming to such a conclusion when confronted by the war's realities. Such views on the need for strong government had an enduring influence on American political thought.

The poet, essayist, and philosopher Ralph Waldo Emerson (1803–1882) was a leading 19th-century intellectual. He was an admirer of President Abraham Lincoln and his policies.

See also
- Abolition
- Brown, John
- Emancipation Proclamation
- Legacy of the Civil War
- Literature

Invention and technology

The Civil War saw major advances in technology. Generals used the electric telegraph to coordinate the movements of vast armies, while both sides faced highly destructive new weapons such as concealed mines and the machine gun.

The great advances in technology made during the war were partly due to the 19th-century enthusiasm for scientific innovation and partly to the belief on both sides that new technology would help them fight the war more efficiently. The war sparked a race among inventors to develop rapid-fire small arms such as breechloading rifles and machine guns. Older types of weapons were used in innovative ways. For example, heavy artillery was mounted on railroad cars, which gave it a new flexibility. The naval war saw the deployment of sea mines (then called torpedoes) and submarines—both developed by the Confederacy during the war to defend its coastline against the Union navy.

The war also exploited the massive potential of some prewar inventions. The sewing machine, invented in 1846, allowed Union factories to clothe vast armies, while the electric telegraph revolutionized military communications.

The telegraph was introduced in the 1840s, and by 1861 a network had spread across the country from east to

Operators constructing telegraph lines at a Union camp in April 1864. During the war over 15,000 miles (24,000km) of lines were laid specifically for military purposes.

west (see box on page 40). Telegraph lines were originally laid alongside railroads to control train movements. During the war they were also laid along the routes of the armies, keeping the war departments in Washington, D.C., and Richmond informed as battles were won and lost. The telegraph allowed Civil War generals to employ strategies on a scale not seen before in war. In May 1864 General-in-chief of the Union army, Ulysses S. Grant, gave daily orders to his armies in Virginia, Georgia, and West Virginia, thus coordinating the operations of more than half a million soldiers.

Infernal machines

The Civil War spurred the development of many of the weapons that went on to dominate warfare in the 20th century. The destructive capability of these new machines horrified contemporaries.

It was the Confederacy, outnumbered by Union forces and desperate to defend every inch of territory, that developed land mines, then also called torpedoes. Mines were first used to halt the Union army's advance during the Peninsular Campaign in 1862. Confederate General Gabriel J. Rains surrounded his tiny garrison at Yorktown with concealed artillery shells that were rigged to be detonated by trip wires and pressure plates. Union General George B. McClellan was outraged: "The rebels," he telegraphed Washington, "have been guilty of the most murderous and barbarous conduct in placing torpedoes [land mines] within abandoned works near wells and springs; near flagstaffs, magazines [and] telegraph offices.... I shall make the prisoners remove them at their own peril."

The rank-and-file on both sides dubbed these concealed mines "infernal machines." But they proved their worth, and the Confederacy allocated more money for their development. By 1864 Rains had been given a budget of $350,000 by the Confederate Congress to lay land mines to defend Richmond. That year he supervised the laying of over 1,200 mines around the city.

Sea mines

The Confederates also developed several types of sea mine to sink Union navy ships. The Russian navy had used sea mines in a limited way during the Crimean War (1853–1856), but in the Civil War they proved their destructive potential. A Civil War sea mine was a watertight cylinder made from tin or sheet-iron and packed with gunpowder. It had an air-filled chamber to give it buoyancy. Sea mines floated just below the water surface and were anchored to the seabed by cable. They could be detonated by an enemy vessel pulling on a trigger wire attached to a float. The most sophisticated device used was

Confederate sea mines (then called torpedoes) in the arsenal yard at Charleston, South Carolina. The first sea mines used during the Civil War were simply floating barrels stuffed with gunpowder.

THE INVENTION OF THE TELEGRAPH

The electric telegraph revolutionized communications around the world in the mid-19th century. In 1825 the British inventor William Sturgeon (1783–1850) exhibited an electromagnet—a bar of iron surrounded by coils of copper wire that could be turned into a magnet by passing an electric current through the wire. The electric signal could be switched on and off, causing the magnet to either press a lever or move a marker. In the United States in the 1830s Samuel F.B. Morse (1791–1872) created a communication system using this signal. It consisted of an operator key and a receiver. When the key was pressed, it completed the electric circuit and sent a signal to the receiver, which turned on the magnet. This then moved a mechanism that made an indentation on a paper roll or, later in the 1850s, made a sound that the operator could listen to. The Morse Code used combinations of short and long signals (dots and dashes) that were decoded by the operator at the receiving end.

In 1844 the first stretch of telegraph line was laid on wooden poles along 35 miles (56km) of railroad track between Washington, D.C., and Baltimore, Maryland. The system began operation on May 24 with the message: "What hath God wrought."

A Union signal telegraph machine and operator at Fredericksburg in 1862, sketched by Alfred Waud.

the electric detonator, which was triggered by wire from shore. It was first used on the Yazoo River, Mississippi, in 1862 to sink the USS *Cairo*. No Civil War sea mine was self-propelled, although there were experiments with such weapons. Instead, mines were attached to vessels by a spar (long wooden pole). The spar was then rammed into an enemy ship. These "spar torpedoes" were fitted to small, fast vessels, converting the boats into destructive warships. By the end of the war Confederate mines had sunk 29 Union vessels and damaged 14, which made the mine the most effective weapon used by the Confederates against the Union navy.

Warships

The naval war also saw the deployment of two of the most innovative types of warship ever built—submarines and ironclads. The Confederate submarine CSS *Hunley* became the first submarine to sink an enemy vessel in wartime when it rammed the USS *Housatonic* with a spar torpedo on February 17, 1864, in Charleston harbor. The *Hunley* and its eight-man crew sank soon after the attack. The reason why remains a mystery.

The USS *Monitor* was a steam-propelled and iron-plated warship, known as an ironclad. It has been called the first modern warship. The *Monitor's* most innovative feature was its rotating iron gun turret. The *Monitor's* designer, John Ericsson, referred to it not as a ship but as a floating gun battery. *Monitor's* battle with the Confederate ironclad CSS *Virginia* in Hampton Roads, Virginia, on March 9, 1862, led the Union navy to commission many ironclad vessels of the same design.

New firearms

One of the major technological advances for Civil War soldiers was the breechloading repeating rifle, because it was quick to load and allowed the user to fire several shots before reloading. The seven-shot Spencer rifle was patented in 1860. More than 12,000 Spencer rifles and 94,000 carbines were bought by the Union government. The Henry was a more advanced rifle, but it was not introduced until the last year of the war, and only 10,000 were issued. The Henry's 15-shot magazine could be emptied in just 11 seconds.

During the war there was a race to invent the first practical machine gun, which would provide rapid, continuous fire. Several types made an appearance during the Civil War. The most famous was patented in 1862 by Richard Gatling of Indianapolis, Indiana.

The Gatling gun

The Gatling was a six-barreled gun that used a rotating mechanism to load, fire, and eject ammunition at a (then) phenomenal rate of 200 rounds per minute. The gun had several serious drawbacks. It was too big and heavy to be maneuverable in rough country and used gunpowder, which produced dense clouds of smoke that obscured the target. These problems were eventually solved by inventors around the world over the next 30 years. During the Civil war only 12 Gatling guns were used by the Union army. They were bought privately by General Benjamin Butler in 1864. Gatling himself sincerely believed his invention would bring an end to war because the carnage his new weapon could inflict would make any future war unthinkable.

See also

• Artillery
• Communications and signals
• Ironclads
• Railroads
• Strategy and tactics
• Submarines
• Transportation
• Weapons and firearms

The 13-inch (33-cm) Union mortar known as the "Dictator" mounted on a railroad car in October 1864 during the Siege of Petersburg, Virginia. Giant mortars were traditionally used in coastal forts. The Union used railroads to transform them into portable guns.

Iowa

Iowa supported the Union cause, and there was strong antislavery feeling in the state. Although no fighting took place on its soil, Iowa provided a greater proportion of its population to the Union army than any other state.

Long before the Civil War the slavery issue played a major role in politics in Iowa. For many years a bastion of the Democrats, Iowa swung emphatically to the Republicans after the party was formed in the state in 1856. Over the

Union troops of the 1st Iowa Regiment, led by Nathaniel Lyon, make a charge at the Battle of Wilson's Creek on August 10, 1861, near Springfield, Missouri.

See also

- Abolition
- Brown, John
- Economy of the North
- Governors, Union
- Politics, Union
- Underground Railroad
- Union army

next five years, as deep splits opened in U.S. society, Iowa remained firmly on the antislavery side of the debate.

Before the war Iowa played an important role in agitating for the emancipation of slaves. Many runaway slaves found their way to freedom in and through Iowa. Numerous Quaker towns in the state served as stations on the so-called Underground Railroad, which was an informal network of guides who helped runaway slaves escape to the North and Canada.

Abolitionist John Brown trained his followers in the Quaker village of Springdale, Iowa, where he had his

headquarters for several years. Some of them later fought with Brown in his 1859 attack on the government arsenal at Harpers Ferry in Virginia.

Answering the call

When President Abraham Lincoln called for troops in 1861 and Governor Samuel J. Kirkwood announced that a regiment must be formed, the state had no trouble filling its quota: Indeed, 10 times the required number of Iowans volunteered. For the greater part of the war every call for further military, political, and financial support for the Union was answered with enthusiasm in the state. It was not until September 1864 that there was any significant opposition to Washington's requests, and the governor of Iowa was forced for the first time to resort to the draft to supply the state quota of soldiers.

Iowans served in Union campaigns throughout the country. About one half of all men of military age in the state served in the army. There were 46 Iowa infantry regiments, 440 African Americans in a black regiment, four batteries of light artillery, nine regiments of cavalry, and thousands of troops in replacement units.

In total more than 76,000 men from Iowa served in the Union army. More than 13,000 died in the conflict, and a further 8,500 Iowan soldiers were seriously wounded.

Ironclads

The development during the Civil War of steam-powered armored warships, known as ironclads, had a great influence on naval warfare. Both sides spent a large amount of time and money developing this revolutionary type of vessel.

The Confederate and Union navy secretaries knew that warships needed iron armor to withstand the powerful new 19th-century artillery. Britain and France each had an ironclad in 1861, but the Civil War hastened the development of these warships, which formed a transitional phase between the old wooden sail-powered warships and the battleships of the late 19th century.

USS *Monitor*

In 1861 Union Secretary of the Navy Gideon Welles commissioned Swedish inventor John Ericsson to build the first Union ironclad. Ericsson completed his revolutionary ship, the USS *Monitor*, in January 1862. Some 172 feet (52m) long and armed with two 11-inch (28-cm) Dahlgren guns in a revolving iron turret, the *Monitor* was technically in advance of any warship afloat when launched. Its armor plating was 8 inches (20cm) thick. Since it was almost impossible to make iron plates this thick, the armor of the *Monitor*, like most later ironclads, was made of 1-inch (2.5-cm) plates bolted together.

The craft had a strange appearance since it had a very low freeboard—the deck of the ship was only 1 foot (30cm) above the waterline. This led it to be dubbed the "Yankee cheesebox on a raft." Its main drawback was that it was barely seaworthy. Nevertheless, the *Monitor* became the pattern for one of the most popular types of ironclad. Of the 52 coastal ironclads contracted for by the Union during the war, 48 were "monitors" that followed this design.

Casemate ironclads

The Union also contracted for 24 ironclads to patrol internal waters. They did not have gun turrets. Instead, they were built with a casemate—an iron-plated box that protected the guns and crew of the ship. Casemate ironclads often had sloping sides, which presented a thicker layer of armor to direct shot. The first of these Union casemate ironclads was

Union officers on board the USS Monitor *on July 9, 1862. Dents can be seen on the gun turret where it was hit during its duel with the CSS* Virginia *in the Battle of Hampton Roads, March 9, 1862.*

The Union casemate ironclad Baron de Kalb *(formerly the* Saint Louis*). It was one of seven ironclads built for use on Western rivers that were known as "Pook Turtles" after their designer, Samuel M. Pook. The* Baron de Kalb *was sunk by a Confederate sea mine in the Yazoo River in 1863.*

launched in October 1861. It was one of seven ironclads designed by Samuel M. Pook for the Union and known as "Pook Turtles." The Pook Turtles contributed to Union victories on Western rivers in 1862 and 1863.

Confederate ironclads

The Confederacy lacked the facilities and resources to build large warships to match those in the Union navy. It had only one major shipyard in New Orleans and one ironworks—Tredegar Ironworks in Richmond, Virginia. However, when Virginia seceded from the Union in 1861, Confederate forces took over the U.S. Navy's Norfolk shipyard in the state. With this action the Confederates gained the U.S. Navy's new steamship, the *Merrimack*, which Union troops had partly burned and sunk before leaving.

Confederate engineers raised the *Merrimack* and built on its hull a large armored casemate. An iron ram was mounted to its bow. The Confederacy named its new casemate ironclad the CSS *Virginia*, and it set sail in March 1862. The *Virginia* was designed to operate both in coastal waters and on rivers. On March 9, 1862, the first ever battle between ironclads took place in Hampton Roads, Virginia, when the USS *Monitor* and CSS *Virginia* pounded each other in a four-hour duel that ended inconclusively.

Ironclad-building programs

The appearance of the CSS *Virginia* briefly brought about "ram fever" in the North—a great fear that Confederate ironclads, known as rams, were about to attack Northern coastal cities. In the South there was much enthusiasm for ironclads, and women in several cities raised funds to build vessels, which were known as "Ladies' Gunboats."

In the fall of 1862 the Confederacy began constructing a remarkable 18 ironclads. The Confederacy also planned to beat the Union with more technically advanced ships built in Europe. At the end of the war two large rams were under construction in England. However, they never reached the Confederacy.

On May 20, 1862, Union forces attacked the Norfolk shipyard to win it back. Confederates sank the *Virginia*, which was trapped there, to prevent it from falling into Union hands. This loss, along with the loss of four other ironclads, and the fall of the ports of New Orleans and Memphis into Union hands proved that expectations of the new vessels had been too high. Enthusiasm in the South had waned by early 1863. In all, the Confederacy completed 22 ironclads during the war while the Union built more than 40. The Union was able to capitalize on its strengths in industry, skilled labor, and access to iron to far outstrip the South in ironclad production.

Jackson, Battle of

The Battle of Jackson, Mississippi, took place on May 14, 1863. It was the third of five significant engagements in Union General Ulysses S. Grant's bid to isolate and surround the Confederate stronghold of Vicksburg, Mississippi.

Jackson, the state capital, was an important transportation hub 38 miles (60km) east of the Confederate river city of Vicksburg. On April 30, 1863, Union General Ulysses S. Grant's Army of the Tennessee began crossing the Mississippi River at Bruinsburg, 30 miles (48km) south of Vicksburg. Although his ultimate objective was Vicksburg, Grant did not advance directly on the city. Instead, he sent his army east to mislead the Confederate commander, John C. Pemberton, and to prevent Pemberton's army from receiving supplies and reinforcements.

Grant's 40,000 troops substantially outnumbered Pemberton's 30,000. On May 9 an alarmed President Jefferson Davis ordered Joseph E. Johnston to take charge of Confederate forces in Mississippi, march to Pemberton's aid, and drive away Grant's army. When Johnston arrived at Jackson four days later, however, he quickly concluded that he had no chance of rescuing Pemberton. Instead, he withdrew his own force, leaving 6,000 men under John Gregg to cover the retreat.

Gregg placed his force just west of Jackson and waited for the Union attack. On May 14 Grant's XVII Corps under James B. McPherson located Gregg's troops and deployed for battle. Meanwhile, William T. Sherman's XV Corps moved up from the south. At 11:00 A.M. McPherson launched his first assault, which drove Gregg's men back to a defensive line near the town. He was preparing a second attack when word arrived that the Confederates had abandoned the field. At 4:00 P.M. Union forces were entering Jackson— the fourth Southern state capital to fall.

Consequences

Although hardly a pitched battle— Confederate losses totaled 850 men, Union losses 300—the engagement had two important results. First, the victory allowed Grant's troops to destroy much of Jackson's railroads and war factories. Second, it meant that Pemberton's army, outnumbered and outgeneraled, had to face Grant alone. The stage was set for Pemberton's defeats at Champion's Hill (May 16) and Big Black River (May 17). Pemberton's army retreated into Vicksburg on May 18 and Grant began to besiege the city.

See also

- Grant, Ulysses S.
- Johnston, Joseph E.
- Mississippi
- Vicksburg, Siege of
- West, the Civil War in the

Union troops of the 17th Iowa, 80th Ohio, and 10th Missouri Regiments charge the Confederate line at the Battle of Jackson, Mississippi, on May 14, 1863.

Jackson, Thomas J.

One of the greatest Confederate commanders, "Stonewall" Jackson (1824–1863) was famous for his brilliant tactics and bold strikes against Union forces. His career was cut short by his untimely death after the Battle of Chancellorsville.

"Stonewall" Jackson became a hero in the Confederacy because of his aggressive tactics and the speed with which he was able to move his troops from place to place.

Thomas Jonathan Jackson was born on January 21, 1824, in Clarksburg, Virginia (now West Virginia). He was orphaned at an early age and was brought up by relatives. Jackson had little formal education until he entered the U.S. Military Academy at West Point in 1842. After graduating in 1846, he fought in the Mexican War (1846–1848), during which he was promoted three times for bravery.

Virginia Military Institute

After the Mexican War Jackson left the army, finding peacetime service unrewarding. In 1851 he was appointed professor of artillery tactics and natural philosophy at the Virginia Military Institute (VMI) in Lexington, where he remained for 10 years. He became a Presbyterian, and his faith had a profound influence on him for the rest of his life—he was sometimes called "Deacon Jackson."

Jackson had several eccentricities; for example, he imagined that one side of his body weighed more than the other

and so often walked or rode with one arm raised to keep his balance. During his time at VMI he married twice. His first wife, Elinor Junkin, died in childbirth. In 1857 he married Mary Anna Morrison, who bore him his only surviving daughter, Julia, in 1862. In 1859 Jackson witnessed the execution of the abolitionist John Brown, when he accompanied a group of VMI cadets to stand guard at the hanging. He later wrote that he was so moved by Brown's plight that he petitioned for his pardon.

Jackson joined the Confederate army when the Civil War started out of loyalty to his home state, Virginia. He earned his nickname of "Stonewall" at Bull Run (Manassas) in July 1861, the first major battle of the war. As his brigade stood firm in the face of a Union onslaught, a fellow officer, General Barnard Bee, rallied his troops by pointing out the conduct of Jackson and his brigade: "There is Jackson, standing like a stone wall!" For his actions Jackson was promoted to major general in October 1861.

Valley campaign

In spring 1862 Jackson led a campaign in the Shenandoah Valley, during which he defeated Union generals whose combined strength was several times his own. His orders were to keep Union General Nathaniel P. Banks from joining forces with General George B.

McClellan, who was fighting the Peninsular Campaign. During the six-week campaign his diversionary tactics succeeded brilliantly. The speed with which Jackson's troops were able to march earned them the nickname of Jackson's "Foot Cavalry."

Jackson then joined Robert E. Lee, who had taken command of Southern forces in Virginia and reorganized them into the Army of Northern Virginia. In the ensuing Seven Days' Campaign of June 1862 Jackson became slow and ineffective, probably due to physical exhaustion. He soon recovered, however, and at Second Bull Run (Manassas) he marched with 20,000 men over 50 miles in two days, destroying the Union supply base at Manassas Junction on August 27. At the battles of Antietam (Sharpsburg) on September 17 and Fredericksburg on December 13 his troops fought hard, making a great contribution to a string of Southern victories. In October 1862 Jackson was promoted to lieutenant

general, and Lee gave him comand of II Corps of the Army of Northern Virginia. The two men worked well together: Jackson said he trusted Lee so much he would follow him blindfolded.

Battle of Chancellorsville
In May 1863 Jackson won his greatest victory at Chancellorsville, Virginia. Lee sent him on a wide flanking march to attack the right wing of Joseph Hooker's Union army from the rear, which Jackson accomplished with devastating effect. But the battle had a tragic aftermath. Returning home from a scouting mission on the evening of May 2, Jackson's party was mistaken for enemy troops, and he was shot by his own men. The wound was not fatal, but his arm had to be amputated. He contracted pneumonia and died eight days later, on May 10, 1863. Jackson's death was a bitter loss for the Confederate cause and particularly for Robert E. Lee, who mourned: "I know not how to replace him."

A drawing entitled "Three Heroes" showing three of the great Confederate commanders: In the center is General Robert E. Lee, flanked by Stonewall Jackson (right) and J.E.B. Stuart (left).

See also

- Antietam (Sharpsburg), Battle of
- Bull Run (Manassas), Second Battle of
- Chancellorsville, Battle of
- Confederate army
- Fredericksburg, Battle of
- Lee, Robert E.
- Lost Cause
- Military academies, North and South
- Northern Virginia, Army of
- Seven Days' Campaign
- Shenandoah Valley

Johnson, Andrew

Andrew Johnson (1808–1875) was elected vice president in November 1864. The following April President Lincoln was assassinated, and Johnson became president. He faced the daunting task of reconstructing the troubled nation.

President Andrew Johnson came into bitter conflict with Congress. He favored a lenient approach toward the defeated South, while Congress wanted to seize the chance to radically reshape the Southern states and grant political rights to the freed slaves.

The timing of Lincoln's assassination, which happened only a few days after the end of the war, gave Andrew Johnson the heavy responsibility of trying to reunite the North and South after four years of war and division. The task destroyed his administration within three years and saw Johnson himself impeached and on trial before the U.S. Senate, charged with gross misconduct. No other U.S. president has suffered such a fate.

Early life

Born in Raleigh, North Carolina, Andrew Johnson came from a poor family and had very little schooling. He began his working life apprenticed to a tailor at the age of 13. Moving to Greeneville, Tennessee, in 1826, he began a tailoring business of his own. He married Eliza McCardle in 1827, and with her help he learned to read and write and then went on to educate himself further and to take part in local debates. His business prospered, and he used his ambition, drive, and gift for public speaking to enter Greeneville politics, becoming a town alderman in 1828 and then mayor in 1830.

A national figure

Success in Greeneville led Johnson into national politics. In 1843 he entered Congress as the Democratic Party's representative for Tennessee. He remained in Congress until 1853 and then returned to Tennessee as governor. He held the post until 1857, when he was elected to the Senate.

In his prewar political career Johnson stood up for the rights of the poor and for small farmers and businessmen, and spoke out against the plantation owners who dominated politics in Tennessee and the rest of the South. He championed the Homestead Bill to grant free land to settlers on the western frontier (the bill was eventually passed into law in 1862).

In the great debate of the 1850s over whether or not slavery should be extended into the new territories, Johnson supported the Southern belief that it should. Although Johnson upheld the institution of slavery, he remained pro-Union and refused to support Southern secession even after Tennessee seceded in May 1861. Johnson was the only senator from a seceded state to remain at his post in Washington, D.C.

Pro-Union Democrat

During the war the Republican President Lincoln recognized Johnson's political usefulness as a pro-Union Southern Democrat. In March 1862, after Union forces had occupied central Tennessee, Lincoln appointed Johnson military governor of the state. Johnson's staunch work for the Union in the face of persistent local hostility, led to his selection as Lincoln's running mate in 1864. Lincoln was reelected, and Johnson became vice president. He held the office for six weeks before Lincoln's assassination on April 14, 1865, made Johnson the new president.

Presidency and impeachment

Johnson tried to continue Lincoln's policy of clemency toward the defeated Confederacy. In this he was opposed by Congress, which was dominated by Radical Republicans who wanted harsher treatment of the former enemy and political rights for the freed slaves. These differing views on how best to reconstruct the South turned into a bitter political fight.

On May 29, 1865, Johnson announced a pardon for many former Confederates before Congress was in session. He also planned to remove the North's military governments in the South and readmit representatives of Southern states to Congress. Johnson, who firmly believed he had the support

of the people, went on to use his presidential veto to thwart several bills passed by Congress. On March 2, 1867, Congress ran out of patience with the president and passed—despite Johnson's veto—a Reconstruction Bill based on military administration of the Southern states and black suffrage. Congress also passed the Tenure of Office Bill, which limited the president's freedom to remove officials. In defiance of this Johnson dismissed Secretary of War Edwin M. Stanton— a Radical Republican—in August 1867. On February 28, 1868, Congress voted to impeach Andrew Johnson on 11 charges of misconduct centering on the firing of Stanton.

Johnson's Senate trial took place between March 5 and April 11, 1868. The charges did not stand up to scrutiny, and the president was acquitted. He continued in office until the end of his term in 1869, but he was almost powerless. Johnson later made two attempts to return to public office before winning a Senate seat in March 1875. He died suddenly on July 31.

Andrew Johnson's impeachment trial in the Senate in spring 1868. Johnson was charged with the illegal firing of Secretary of War Edwin M. Stanton.

See also

- Black Codes
- Democratic Party
- Election of 1864
- Lincoln, Abraham
- Lincoln's assassination
- Reconstruction
- Republican Party
- Tennessee

Johnston, Albert S.

At the beginning of the Civil War Albert Sidney Johnston (1803–1862) was one of the most promising Confederate generals. His friend President Jefferson Davis saw his decision to fight for the Southern cause as a sure sign of victory.

Johnston was wounded in the leg at the Battle of Shiloh on April 6, 1862. He ignored the wound and bled to death.

Born in Kentucky in 1803, Albert Sidney Johnston graduated from the U.S. Military Academy at West Point in 1826. He served in the U.S. Army until 1834, when he resigned to care for his dying wife.

After his wife's death in 1836 Johnston went to Texas to fight in the revolution against Mexico. By 1838 he had risen to army commander and then secretary of war for the Republic of Texas. During the Mexican War (1846–1848) he led the 1st Texas Rifles as colonel, and his success led him to return to the regular U.S. Army service. He became colonel of the 2nd Cavalry in 1855, and after a campaign into Utah against the Mormons in 1857 he was promoted to the brevet rank of brigadier general. Johnston was serving in California when the Civil War broke out in April 1861.

Johnston resigned from the U.S. Army after Texas seceded and traveled to Richmond, taking four months to make the journey. President Jefferson Davis then gave him command of all Confederate forces west of the Appalachian Mountains to the Mississippi River. Johnston held a defensive line in Kentucky until January 1862. However, his subordinates' defeat at the Battle of Mill Springs on January 19 and the loss of Forts Henry and Donelson in February forced him to abandon Kentucky and most of Tennessee to the Union.

Fatal wound

Johston's reputation was tarnished by these failures, but he rallied his forces in northern Mississippi and launched a counteroffensive into southwest Tennessee in April. He took the Union army of General Ulysees S. Grant completely by surprise in an attack at Pittsburg Landing on the Tennessee River on April 6. The Battle of Shiloh, as it is known, was Johnston's last fight. In the afternoon, directing his troops near the front line, he was shot in the leg. He ignored the wound and slowly bled to death. His death at Shiloh was a great loss felt by his army and the whole Confederacy.

See also

Johnston, Joseph E.

Joseph Eggleston Johnston (1807–1891) was the only general to command, at one time or another, every major Confederate army. He was valued for his skill as a defensive strategist although he was sometimes thought too cautious.

Born on February 3, 1807, in Farmville, Virginia, Johnston was the grandnephew of the American revolutionary Patrick Henry. After graduating from the U.S. Military Academy at West Point in 1829, Johnston participated in the Second Seminole War in Florida (1835–1842) and the Mexican War (1846–1848). In 1860 he was appointed quartermaster general of the U.S. Army.

Johnston was the highest-ranking officer to resign his commission in the U.S. Army on the outbreak of war. He entered Confederate service as a brigadier general—then the highest rank in the Confederate army. Johnston was placed in command of all forces in Virginia following success at the First Battle of Bull Run (Manassas) in July 1861. In May 1862 he was wounded at the Battle of Fair Oaks (Seven Pines) and replaced by Robert E. Lee.

Relationship with Davis

In November 1862 Confederate President Jefferson Davis placed the recuperating Johnston in command of the Department of the West. Johnston oversaw two Confederate armies, one based at Chattanooga, Tennessee, and the other at Vicksburg, Mississippi. Johnston and Davis disagreed over how best to defend Vicksburg from the Union. The town surrendered on July 4, 1863, and Johnston was unfairly blamed by Davis for the loss. The relationship between the two men deteriorated even further as the war went on.

Johnston next commanded the Confederate Army of Tennessee in its effort to turn back Union General William T. Sherman's forces advancing south toward Atlanta, Georgia, in May 1864.

Davis grew impatient with Johnston's defensive strategy and relieved him of command in July in favor of John Bell Hood. Atlanta fell to the Union in any case, and Johnston returned to duty in March 1865 at the request of Robert E. Lee. Johnston had initial success at Bentonville, North Carolina (March 19–21), but he had too few men to achieve a decisive result and soon realized that it was hopeless to resist further. On April 17 Johnston met with Sherman to negotiate surrender.

After the war Johnston served as a congressman and then as commissioner of railroads. He died of pneumonia on March 21, 1891.

Joseph E. Johnston was the highest-ranking officer in the U.S. Army to resign on the outbreak of war.

See also

- Bull Run (Manassas), First Battle of
- Chattanooga, Battle of
- Confederate army
- Fair Oaks, Battle of
- March to the Sea and the Carolinas Campaign
- Surrender of the Confederacy
- Vicksburg, Siege of

Jonesboro, Battle of

The Battle of Jonesboro was the last battle in Union General William T. Sherman's campaign to capture Atlanta, Georgia. On August 31 and September 1, 1864, Sherman's forces fought John Bell Hood's Confederate Army of Tennessee.

Union forces attacking the outnumbered Confederates led by William J. Hardee at the Battle of Jonesboro, just outside Atlanta, Georgia, on September 1, 1864.

At the end of July 1864 John Bell Hood's Confederate army had retreated into Atlanta and was being bombarded by Union General William T. Sherman's forces. Sherman realized that the city was too strongly defended to be taken by direct assault. On August 25 he withdrew most of his army, moving them to cut the railroads west and south of Atlanta. If he could cut the Confederates' supply line, they would be forced out of the city. Hood interpreted Sherman's movements as a retreat. When he received reports of Union troops near Jonesboro, just south of Atlanta on the Macon and Western Railroad, he figured them to be only a raiding party and sent troops under William J. Hardee to destroy them. Hood's failure to perceive the danger facing him had dire consequences.

On August 31 Hardee was surprised to encounter not raiders but virtually the entire Union force near Jonesboro. Six Union army corps had moved in an arc around the Atlanta defenses. Hardee made an uncoordinated and ineffective attack, and the Confederates suffered high casualties with no success. This failure forced the other Confederate corps, under Stephen D. Lee, back to a defensive position along the Macon and Western Railroad. On September 1 Sherman cut the railroad north of Jonesboro, then attacked again in the afternoon, forcing Lee to retreat. Once the last supply line was cut, Hood's Confederates were forced to evacuate Atlanta. They left on the night of September 1, and Union troops entered the city the next day.

Confederate defeat

The Battle of Jonesboro and the subsequent loss of Atlanta removed any doubt that the Confederacy would be defeated. Sherman's forces suffered 1,150 casualties at Jonesboro, and a total of 35,000 for the entire Atlanta campaign, but they had given Lincoln the victory that he badly needed. The mismanaged attacks at Jonesboro also showed the command failures that plagued the Confederate Army of Tennessee. The fighting men's valor was wasted time and again in fruitless assaults such as that at Jonesboro.

Kansas

Kansas entered the Union as the 34th state on January 29, 1861, less than three months before the Civil War started. The question of whether Kansas would be a free or slave state was one of the issues that led to the conflict.

Kansas was a frontier society in the 1860s. Most of the population of 100,000 were farmers. There were only 10 towns with a population of more than 500 people. The Missouri Compromise of 1820 had determined that new territories north of latitude 36° 30' could not be slave-owning. In 1854 the Kansas–Nebraska Act created the territories of Kansas and Nebraska from what had been Indian Territory. Although Kansas lay north of 36° 30', the act allowed its residents to decide whether it should be free or slave. Both pro- and antislavery supporters came to Kansas, where the dispute developed into an issue of national importance.

The Kansas–Nebraska Act

The Kansas–Nebraska Act, put forward by Stephen A. Douglas, an Illinois senator, in effect repealed the Missouri Compromise, allowing the slavery question to be decided by popular vote, or "popular sovereignty," in the new territories. Antislavery settlers in the state believed they outnumbered proslavers and could keep slavery out of Kansas by the vote. However, the first election for a Kansas congressional delegate, held in November 1854, was fraudulent: Proslavery supporters poured over the border from Missouri and voted illegally to win the election. A subsequent election, to elect territorial representatives, was also won fraudulently. The illegally elected new government then passed legislation to allow and promote slavery in the state.

The response from antislavery supporters was swift and forceful. Eli Thayer formed the New England Emigrant Aid Company and sent 1,200 armed New Englanders to settle new land. The abolitionist minister Henry Ward Beecher supplied abolitionist settlers with Sharps rifles, known as "Beecher's Bibles." In opposition to the illegal proslavery government the free-staters, who wanted a free-labor state, set up their own government in the territory.

The proslavery Southern government was based at Lecompton and the free-state government at Topeka. Confusion ensued as to which government was legitimate. A congressional committee was sent from Washington, D.C., to investigate the situation. Although the committee found that the elections were fraudulent, the U.S. government failed to take action to remove the proslavery government.

An illustrated sheet music cover for an antislavery song. It features a roundel of the burning of the Free State Hotel in Lawrence, Kansas, by a proslavery mob in May 1856.

The main street in Atchinson, Kansas, in the early 1860s, one of the very few towns in the new state. Immigration into Kansas stopped during the Civil War.

Bleeding Kansas

Violence quickly broke out between the opposing political factions. Throughout eastern Kansas abolitionists and free-staters fought against proslavers. As a result of the violence, the period became known as "Bleeding Kansas."

Many proslavery supporters tried to force free-staters out of the territory by intimidation, which rapidly turned to violence in the form of kidnappings and killings. As the violence escalated, the antislavery town of Lawrence was raided. Five people were killed, and a hotel, printing presses, stores, and homes were burned by forces from Missouri. In retaliation the abolitionist John Brown and his four sons brutally hacked to death five unarmed, proslavery men at Pottawatomie Creek.

In another large-scale action James Montgomery led free-state forces to effectively drive antislavery forces from Linn County, Kansas. Proslavery forces retaliated by snatching 11 free-staters from their homes and shooting them in a ravine. The killings were known as the Marais de Cygnes Massacre. Raids and skirmishes continued up to the admission of Kansas into the Union as a free state on January 29, 1861, and the start of the Civil War in April.

Kansas troops

Most Kansans supported the Union. Of the 30,000 men of military age 20,000 joined federal forces, and some of the first African American regiments were raised in the state. Military action started mainly as a series of skirmishes and raids along the Missouri border. The first serious engagement of Kansas forces was at the Battle of Wilson's Creek near Springfield, Missouri, on August 10, 1861. Kansas forces participated in further campaigns in Kentucky, Tennessee, and Mississippi, and with Ulysses S. Grant at Vicksburg. The state suffered 8,500 casualties.

Military action

On August 21, 1863, Confederate guerrillas led by William C. Quantrill attacked Lawrence, killing about 200 people and burning 200 buildings. The first large-scale military engagement took place in the fall of 1864, when 12,000 Confederates under Sterling Price marched north to seize St. Louis, Missouri, and rally support for their cause. They were pushed into Kansas by Union forces. Battles took place at Lexington, at the Big and Little Blue Rivers, and at Westport. As Price retreated south, he attempted to capture Fort Scott, Kansas, a Union supply center, but he was defeated at the Battle of Mine Creek by 10,000 Kansas militia and regular troops. The victory saved Kansas from any further invasion from the South.

Kansas–Nebraska Act

The Kansas–Nebraska Act was a crucial point in the sequence of events leading to the Civil War. The act came into force on May 30, 1854, and allowed settlers in new U.S. territory to decide for themselves whether they would permit slavery.

In 1853 Senator Stephen A. Douglas of Illinois introduced a bill in Congress to organize a new territory, Nebraska. Douglas, a rising star in the Democratic Party, hoped that the creation of the new territory would be the first step toward the construction of a transcontinental railroad that would connect his hometown of Chicago with California. Southern congressmen blocked the bill because they hoped for a southern route for the railroad. Needing Southern support, Douglas revised the bill to create two new territories, Kansas and Nebraska. The bill provided that settlers who moved to the new territories would be allowed to decide for themselves whether Kansas and Nebraska would permit slavery. Douglas called this "popular sovereignty." Many assumed that Nebraska would vote against slavery, while Kansas, which bordered slaveholding Missouri, would permit it.

Strong reaction

The bill was passed by Congress in May 1854 by a vote of 115 to 104. The reaction was immediate and fierce. Antislavery Northern congressmen were outraged because the bill potentially opened up Northern territories to slavery. Furthermore, the bill repealed the Missouri Compromise, which for 30 years had preserved the balance of power between the North and South by providing that new states north of the 36° 30' line be admitted as free states and states south of the line become slave states. The impact of the act can be clearly seen in the fall congressional elections of 1854: The number of northern Democrats in the House of Representatives fell from 92 to 23. Opponents of the act elected 150 congressmen.

By 1856 most of the political forces opposed to the act had reorganized themselves into the new Republican Party. The act continued to provide a rallying point for antislavery forces, and thus it led to the triumph of Republican Abraham Lincoln in the presidential elections of 1860, which in turn brought on secession and the Civil War.

In Kansas itself the act resulted in years of violence, a period known as "Bleeding Kansas," as pro- and antislavery settlers struggled for control. Kansas was finally admitted to the Union as a free state in 1861.

See also

- Causes of the conflict
- Democratic Party
- Kansas
- Missouri Compromise
- Republican Party
- Slavery

A political cartoon of 1854 depicts Liberty "the fair maid of Kansas" being mistreated by the "border ruffians." The cartoon criticises the administration for the violence in Kansas that followed the Kansas–Nebraska Act of 1854.

Kennesaw Mountain, Battle of

After a month of maneuvering through Georgia Confederate General Joseph E. Johnston's army made a stand at Kennesaw Mountain near Marietta, Georgia, where it was attacked by William T. Sherman's Union troops on June 27, 1864.

A view of Kennesaw Mountain, near Marietta, Georgia. Confederate General Joseph E. Johnston established an 8-mile (12-km) defensive line that included the slopes of the mountain.

See also

- Atlanta, Fall of
- Infantry tactics
- Johnston, Joseph E.
- Sherman, William T.

On May 5, 1864, Sherman and his three Union armies, totaling nearly 100,000 men, began moving south out of Tennessee toward Atlanta, Georgia. Johnston's 60,000 Confederate troops tried to block the Union advance by entrenching across its path and inviting an assault against their prepared defenses. The campaign became one of maneuver as Sherman moved to get behind Johnston, and the latter shifted to block him. For a month the two forces moved deeper into Georgia as they battled each other, yet Sherman avoided committing his troops to a full attack. Instead, he used his superior numbers to turn Johnston out of his defenses. By mid-June Johnston's troops had fallen back to a ridgeline anchored by Kennesaw Mountain, west of Marietta, Georgia. Believing that Johnston's line was stretched too thin, Sherman decided to attack.

Union attack

At dawn on June 27 Union forces advanced toward the well-entrenched Confederates. Diversionary attacks against the Confederate flanks had little effect. An assault against Pigeon Hill, south of Kennesaw Mountain, was met by deadly fire, forcing the attackers to withdraw. The main assault occurred just south of Pigeon Hill, where 8,000 Union troops were ordered to advance at a run using only fixed bayonets. The advance soon degenerated into confusion as men were halted by concentrated fire from the earthworks to their front. By noon Sherman's men could take no more. The battle had proved to be a disaster. Union casualties for the day totaled 3,000; Confederate losses were 552.

After the battle Sherman decided to return to his strategy of maneuver, flanking Johnston to the west and racing for the Chattahoochie River and Atlanta. Johnston had no choice but to move south, hoping once again to entice Sherman into battle on ground favorable to defense.

Kentucky

Kentucky was a slave state, but was also loyal to the Union. The people found themselves deeply divided about secession. Both sides saw Kentucky as a key to success; its importance prevented it from remaining neutral.

Kentucky was one of the four slave states in the upper South that became known as the border states (the others were Delaware, Maryland, and Missouri). In 1860 Kentucky was a leading producer of hemp and tobacco, both of which depended on slave labor. The state had a total population of 1,150,000, of whom 225,000 were slaves and 10,000 were free blacks. Pro-South and pro-North feelings were evenly balanced in the state, and for decades it had tried to work for a compromise on the issue of slavery. The war brought some of the deepest and bitterest divisions of the conflict to the people of Kentucky.

Strategic state

Both the Union and Confederacy saw control of Kentucky as vital. President Abraham Lincoln (who was Kentucky-born) acknowledged its importance to the Union's survival in 1861. "I think to lose Kentucky," he said "is nearly the same as to lose the whole game. [If] Kentucky is gone we cannot hold Missouri, nor, as I think, Maryland."

The Confederacy saw Kentucky as equally important. Winning the state would secure a northwestern border that would lie between the Appalachian Mountains and the Mississippi River. Such a border would serve as a block against any Union invasion across the Ohio River from Illinois, Indiana, or Ohio south toward Tennessee. In addition it would help keep a route open for Confederate forces to enter Missouri, another border state.

At first the ambitions of North and South to secure Kentucky were frustrated by Governor Beriah Magoffin. He understood how deeply his state was divided and what damage a war would do, so he tried to keep it out of the conflict. He refused Lincoln's call for troops on April 15, 1861, and declared Kentucky neutral on May 20, advising Kentuckians not to enlist on either side. That was an impossible hope. Both the Confederacy and the Union established army camps just outside Kentucky's borders, while inside the state Union government agents began distributing guns to

Fort Anderson, near Paducah, Kentucky, and the Union army camp of the 6th Illinois Cavalry in April 1862.

John Hunt Morgan's Confederate cavalry raiders bivouac in Paris, Kentucky, after levying contributions from the town's inhabitants in 1862.

companies of newly formed Union home guards to counter the pro-South Kentucky state militia. In August 1861 Unionists won control of the state legislature, and the Union government opened an army camp inside Kentucky.

Invasion

War finally broke out in September when both sides invaded the state. On September 3 Confederate General Gideon Pillow advanced from Tennessee and occupied Columbus. The next day a Union force crossed the lower Ohio River into Kentucky and seized the town of Paducah. By September 18 the state legislature had reluctantly abandoned neutrality and declared Kentucky for the Union. Meanwhile, Confederate troops advanced into the east of the state and seized the rail junction at the town of Bowling Green.

By October the Confederates held southern Kentucky from Columbus to the mountains. They organized a rival state government at Bowling Green, which voted to secede, and so on

December 10 Kentucky was admitted to the Confederacy. The state was now split in two, with two governments backed by two opposing armies.

In January 1862 the Union moved to clear out the Confederates. The Battle of Mill Springs on January 19 broke the center of the Confederate position. The fall of Forts Henry and Donelson, which controlled the Confederate defensive line from Columbus to Bowling Green, to Union General Ulysses S. Grant in February forced the Confederates to retreat into Tennessee. On March 2 the garrison at Columbus was evacuated. Kentucky was lost to the Confederacy.

Confederate raids

The South did not give up the fight for Kentucky, however. Confederate cavalry raids by John Hunt Morgan from July 1862 kept the morale of Confederate Kentuckians high and increased Union insecurities. In September Confederate generals Braxton Bragg and Kirby Smith launched a fresh invasion from Tennessee. By October 4 Bragg secured the state capital of Frankfort and set up a new Confederate state government. It was shortlived. At the Battle of Perryville on October 8 a Union army led by Don Carlos Buell met Bragg and forced the Confederate forces back once again into Tennessee.

The last Southern invasion of Kentucky was over, but the state was never totally secure for the Union. John Hunt Morgan and Nathan Bedford Forrest both led cavalry raids into the state over the next two years, and pro-Southern guerrillas made sure that the Union could only maintain order by imposing martial law, which was not lifted until October 1865.

Ku Klux Klan

In the aftermath of the Civil War a number of secret societies sprang up in the defeated Confederacy whose aim was to ensure the continuation of white rule. The Ku Klux Klan was the best known of these white supremacist organizations.

The Ku Klux Klan first made its appearance at Pulaski, Tennessee, in early 1866. At the outset it was apparently just a high-spirited fraternal organization set up by a few former Confederate army officers. The name was taken from the Greek word *kyklos* ("circle"), with the Scottish "clan," spelled with a "k," tacked on at the end simply because it sounded right. Very early in its existence, however, the activities of the Klan took a menacing turn. It became closely connected with the underground Southern movement to restore white supremacy. Groups of Klan members began to intimidate the black population.

Growing organization

Local klans sprang up throughout Tennessee and further afield. In April 1867 a general organization of these local klans was established at a convention held in Nashville. Civil War hero General Nathan Bedford Forrest was reputed to be the first supreme leader of this self-appointed "Invisible Empire of the South."

Most Klan leaders were former Confederate officers who refused to accept the new political order that the Radical Republicans were determined to impose on the defeated South. The fundamental issue was civil rights for newly freed African Americans, in particular, voting rights. The prime purpose of the Klan's activities was to frighten blacks away from the voting booth.

Political background

Immediately after the war a number of Southern states had passed Black Codes, which aimed to make sure that white supremacy continued by restricting the activities of African Americans. The Black Codes denied African Americans the vote, as well as several other rights. Radical Republicans were appalled by the measures. In response they used their majority in Congress to push through Reconstruction legislation that banned Black Codes and imposed military rule across the South to ensure compliance.

This was the backdrop to the increasingly high-profile activities of the Klan during the late 1860s. Any pretense that it was a nonpolitical social

A photograph of Ku Klux Klan members taken in about 1870. They wear hats with "KKK" on them and a skull and bones arranged on the floor in front of them.

REVIVING THE KKK

A reborn Ku Klux Klan organization gained national notoriety during the 1920s. This time the targets were widened to include Roman Catholics, Jews, and foreigners of any sort, especially if they were suspected of being communists or socialists. Because it tapped into so many fears and prejudices, the revived Klan gained wide support, and by 1925 its membership reached four million. It was in a position to elect state officials in places as far apart as Texas and Oregon. The Klan leadership was hit by a series of scandals, however, which saw its support rapidly

dwindle. The Great Depression and World War II finished off this version of the Klan, which was disbanded in 1944.

In the 1950s the emergence of the Civil Rights movement resulted in a revival of Ku Klux Klan organizations in the South. This new Klan was more like the original one, in that it aimed to prevent black voter registration. Its terrorist tactics left it completely discredited as well as unsuccessful. Where the Klan lives on today, it feeds mainly on the hatred of the federal government that is characteristic of survivalist cults.

An illustration showing a man being protected by a federal guard from a mob of supporters of the Ku Klux Klan armed with whips and pistols.

organization was gone—it was right in the front line of resistance to the Radical Republicans, and it enjoyed wide support. Groups of Klansmen rode around at night wearing masks and

white robes terrorizing blacks and also any whites who were seen to be supporting the Radical Republicans. They muffled their horses' hooves so that they could undertake their night raids in eerie silence. Burning crosses added to the terrifying supernatural effect. Where fear alone proved insufficient, they dragged their victims from their beds and interrogated, beat, tortured, and even lynched them.

Decline of the Klan

By 1869 Forrest had had enough of the Klan's atrocities and officially disbanded the organization. Federal laws were passed in 1870s to curb its activities. From this time on the Klan went into decline, although it was revived in a different guise in the 1920s. However, the Klan had largely achieved its aims. It had played an important part in the successful resistance by the South to black civil rights. A further century of white supremacy and black oppression was its legacy.

Lanier, Sidney

The poet and musician Sidney Lanier (1842–1881) fought in the Confederate army. His novels and poetry published after the war expressed a sense of loss and a nostalgia for the Old South, which echoed the feelings of many Southerners.

Sidney Lanier was born in Macon, Georgia, on February 3, 1842. He grew up in a well-to-do family surrounded by music, and he mastered a variety of instruments at an early age. He graduated from Oglethorpe College at age 19 and took a teaching post there. When Georgia seceded from the Union in 1861, Lanier enlisted as a private in the Macon Volunteers.

War service

For most of the war Lanier served alongside his younger brother Clifford, three times refusing a commission so as not to be separated from him. He carried his flute with him throughout the war, entertaining his comrades and finding some solace from the conflict in music. Lanier fought in the battles of Fair Oaks (Seven Pines) and Drewry's Bluffs, and in the Seven Days' Battles around Richmond. He and his brother also survived the Battle of Malvern Hill.

The Lanier brothers were finally separated in 1864 when they served on ships running the Northern blockade.

Sidney's ship was captured, and he was sent as a prisoner of war to Point Lookout, Maryland. There he contracted tuberculosis, which would eventually cause his death in 1881. Although horrified by the realities of war, Lanier was positive about rebuilding the nation after the war. His first novel, *Tiger Lilies,* was published in 1867. In it he described war as a "strange, enormous, terrible flower" and hoped that "this seed might perish in the germ, utterly out of sight and life and memory."

Lanier faced financial problems until 1874, when he became a flutist in the Peabody Symphony Orchestra in Baltimore. He won national recognition in 1875, with the publication of his poems "The Symphony" and "Corn." Much of his poetry was linked to life in the South, and he was deeply aware of the hardships facing his fellow Southerners. As he wrote to a friend, "With us of the younger generation of the South, since the war, pretty much the whole of life has been not dying."

Sidney Lanier was an idealistic poet whose main themes were love and nature. His poetry was strongly influenced by music.

See also

- Blockades and blockade-runners
- Literature
- Lost Cause
- Prisoner-of-war camps
- Reconstruction
- Surrender of the Confederacy

Lee, Robert E.

Confederate General Robert E. Lee (1807–1870) endures in the American memory as perhaps the country's most beloved and revered soldier. From May 1862 he commanded the most famous Confederate army, the Army of Northern Virginia.

Right: A portrait of Robert E. Lee in 1838, when he was a 31-year-old lieutenant in the U.S. Army's prestigious Corps of Engineers.

Born into a prominent Virginia family on January 19, 1807, Robert Edward Lee was the son of General "Light Horse Harry" Lee, one of George Washington's subordinates in the American Revolution. Henry Lee's career after the Revolution was marred by scandal and debt, and Robert's boyhood home, Stratford Hall, passed to another Lee relative. Robert moved with his mother, Ann Hill Carter Lee, to a small home in Alexandria, Virginia. His father died soon afterward in 1818. An appointment to the U.S. Military Academy at West Point in 1825 set the course of Lee's life. He flourished at West Point and graduated second in his class in 1829 with the distinction (held to this day) of being the only Academy graduate to finish without a single demerit for misconduct. After West Point he was commissioned into the prestigious Corps of Engineers. As a lieutenant and then a captain of engineers, Lee worked on improving various fortifications and harbors.

Marriage and Mexico

In June 1830 Lee married Mary Ann Randolph Custis, which connected him by marriage to the family of George Washington (Mary was the daughter of Martha Washington's grandson) and cemented his position in the Virginia aristocracy. The marriage was a happy one and produced seven children.

At the outbreak of the Mexican War (1846–1848) Lee accompanied General Winfield Scott's expedition to Vera Cruz

Below: Stratford Hall, Virginia, the boyhood home of Robert E. Lee. The plantation was built by his great-grandfather, Thomas Lee, in the 1730s.

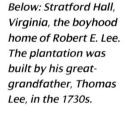

in Mexico, earning battlefield distinction for scouting and staff work. He was promoted for bravery on three occasions and returned to the United States in 1848 as one of the nation's premier young officers and a protégé of Scott, who became the commanding general of the U.S. Army. Lee served for three years as the superintendent of West Point and in 1855 received a permanent promotion to lieutenant colonel. Transferred to Texas, he served as second-in-command of a cavalry regiment until the outbreak of the Civil War in 1861. Scott called Lee to Washington, D.C., and on April 18 offered him command of United States armies forming against the rebellious Southern states.

Agonizing decision

The split between North and South, combined with his expected role in suppressing the rebellion, put Lee in a very difficult position. Lee's family owned slaves and was one of Virginia's oldest and most eminent. When Virginia joined the Confederacy in April, he reached the agonizing, but for him unavoidable, decision to resign from the U.S. Army. He did so on April 20, citing in a letter to Scott his inability to raise his sword against his family and state. Lee was immediately placed in command of Virginia's army and navy. When Virginia's forces came under the control of the Confederate government, Lee was appointed brigadier general, one of the five original Confederate general officers.

After a short, unsuccessful field command in western Virginia and an inspection tour of coastal fortifications in South Carolina and Georgia Lee returned to Richmond to become chief

military advisor to Confederate President Jefferson Davis. After Joseph E. Johnston was wounded in fighting against an advancing Union army, Lee assumed command of Confederate forces defending Richmond. His creation of the Army of Northern Virginia in June 1862 cemented his path to military glory.

Lee's tactics

Upon assuming command, Lee began to use the tactics that would frustrate Northern hopes in the eastern theater of war for the next two years. Most of Lee's battles involved an attempt to fix the enemy in position and at the same time maneuver parts of his army to outflank and destroy his opponent. Lee used a decentralized style of command in which he issued his subordinates overall guidance and left them to accomplish battlefield victory.

In June 1862 Lee immediately took the initiative, defeating General George B. McClellan's Union Army of the Potomac in the Seven Days' Battles and thus saving the Confederate capital of Richmond, Virginia. After dealing with

Robert E. Lee leads his troops at the Battle of Chancellorsville, Virginia, in May 1863. Many consider this battle, in which Lee defeated a Union army twice his size in a series of daring maneuvers, to be his greatest tactical victory.

McClellan, he turned his attention to John Pope's Union Army of Virginia, marching north and crushing it at the Second Battle of Bull Run (August 29–30, 1862). This string of victories compelled Lee to attempt his first invasion of Northern territory in September 1862. He suffered a tactical stalemate at the hands of George B. McClellan at the Battle of Antietam on September 17 and had to retreat back to Virginia. Lee then dealt the Union stinging defeats at Fredericksburg (December 1862) and Chancellorsville (May 1863). His aggressive methods continued to result in victories, but at a high cost in casualties.

Gettysburg and after

Ever mindful of growing Union numerical superiority and the limits of Confederate manpower and resources, Lee determined once again to invade Northern territory in June 1863, hoping to gain military and political advantage. At Gettysburg on July 1-3 he suffered a major defeat, an expensive setback that forever robbed the Army of Northern Virginia of its offensive striking power. From then on Lee was constrained to a war on the defensive, aiming to prevent any Union victory in the east and in this way influence the upcoming 1864 Union presidential election.

From May 1864 Lee waged a titanic campaign against the adversary who finally defeated him, Union General Ulysses S. Grant. Grant's Overland Campaign in Virginia slowly wore down the Army of Northern Virginia and reduced both it and its general to shadows of their former selves. After besieging Richmond and Petersburg from the summer of 1864, Grant's army broke through the Petersburg

fortifications in the first days of April 1865, forcing Lee to evacuate the Confederate capital and leading to his surrender at Appomattox Court House on April 9, 1865.

Postwar years

For the rest of his life Lee served as an example of reconciliation and leadership for all Americans, working to heal the wounds of civil war. He was elected president of Washington College in Lexington, Virginia, in August 1865. His personal example revived the fortunes of the small school (it was later renamed Washington and Lee University in his honor).

After his death in 1870 Lee was revered and mythologized by Southern "Lost Cause" advocates, but he is also loved and honored worldwide as both a great soldier and a good man, one of history's outstanding commanders.

A postwar photograph of Robert E. Lee. After the war ended, he became president of Washington College, in Lexington, Virginia. He set a great example by refusing to express any bitterness and working hard for the country's reconciliation.

See also

Legacy of the Civil War

The war preserved the Union but brought profound changes to the restored nation. Wartime emergencies caused President Lincoln to use his executive power in unprecedented ways, most importantly to emancipate the slaves.

The most immediate and obvious legacy of the Civil War was that it preserved the Union. At the beginning of the war President Abraham Lincoln repeatedly said that saving the Union was his only reason for fighting and that the war was not being fought to free the slaves. That changed over the course of the war, but saving the Union remained foremost among Union war aims, and it was achieved when the Confederate army surrendered in 1865.

Perpetual Union

The Civil War ended a debate that had plagued the nation since its formation in 1776 over whether states could voluntarily secede from the Union, just as the original 13 states had voluntarily joined it when they ratified the Constitution. After the Civil War the doctrine of secession was discredited; it has not since received serious consideration as an acceptable response to real or alleged wrongs done to a state. The Union is now accepted by Americans as permanent. Prior to the Civil War Americans commonly spoke of their nation in the plural: "these United States." After the war the nation became "the United States," suggesting that a loose collection of semi-autonomous states had been replaced by a system in which the states were more like subdivisions of one united country.

Strengthening federal government

The Civil War did not merely preserve the old pre-1861 Union. The war fundamentally changed the relationship between the federal government and the states. The Lincoln administration used federal power in ways that affected people's daily lives as no previous administration had. Congress passed the country's first income tax in

The Capitol building in Washington, D.C. The building was half-finished when the war began. President Lincoln decided to continue with the building work as a symbol that the Union would survive.

1861. It followed that with the Homestead Act of 1862, which granted free land to encourage settlement on the western frontier. The nation's system of banking and finance was modernized and centralized with the passage of the National Banking Act of 1863. That same year Congress passed the nation's first conscription law—also known as the draft—to add manpower to the Union armies.

Lincoln personally exercised more power than previous presidents, especially through the use of executive orders. He used these orders to crack down on those suspected of disloyalty to the Union. Many of Lincoln's actions were viewed as temporary measures made necessary by the emergency of the war, but they set important precedents. The changes in finance and banking remained more or less permanent; the income tax legislation was reenacted on a permanent basis in the early 20th century; the draft became an accepted part of American life for much of that century; and future presidents used executive orders extensively.

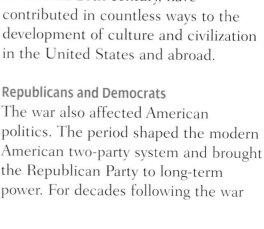

The Lincoln Memorial in Washington, D.C. Many Americans view Abraham Lincoln as the savior of the Union. Many of his executive wartime decisions shaped the political legacy of the Civil War.

The most famous of Lincoln's wartime executive orders was the Emancipation Proclamation, announced in the fall of 1862 and put into action on January 1, 1863. The idea that the president could free millions of slaves with an executive order was unthinkable before the war.

The end of slavery

Although the destruction of slavery was not the original aim of the Lincoln administration, the emancipation of nearly four million African American slaves became the major legacy of the war. The importance of that legacy lay not only in the fact of emancipation but also in the way it came about. More than 180,000 black men served in the Union military and thus played an important role in emancipation.

Wartime military service for African Americans enhanced their status in the postwar nation. The war also helped train a generation of postwar black leaders. The migration of African Americans to the North in the 20th century transformed Northern cities. Freedom did not bring an end to poverty and inequality for African Americans. However, emancipation unleashed the potential of millions of former slaves and their descendants, who, armed with education and empowered by the Civil Rights struggle of the mid-20th century, have contributed in countless ways to the development of culture and civilization in the United States and abroad.

Republicans and Democrats

The war also affected American politics. The period shaped the modern American two-party system and brought the Republican Party to long-term power. For decades following the war

political loyalties reflected the party alignments that had emerged in the late 1850s. The Democratic Party was the dominant party of the South, while the Republican Party remained an almost exclusively Northern party. By the 1930s, however, the Democratic Party was the party of the underprivileged. The Civil Rights movement of the mid-20th century continued the political battles begun during the turmoil of the Reconstruction years (1865–1877).

Constitutional amendments

The war left important legal and constitutional legacies. Chief among them are the three amendments added to the U. S. Constitution as a result of emancipation and Reconstruction. The Thirteenth Amendment (1865) permanently abolished slavery everywhere in the nation. The Fourteenth Amendment (1868) provided that the rights of citizenship

could not be denied without due process of law, and the Fifteenth Amendment (1870) specifically extended the right to vote to African American men. For a century or more following the passage of these amendments Southern states found ways to prevent their enforcement. Civil Rights activists of the 1950s and 1960s used these amendments to fight for equality. The Fourteenth Amendment in particular provided the legal basis for many civil rights court decisions. For example, the "equal protection" clause was the basis for the 1954 *Brown v. Board of Education* decision outlawing school segregation.

Economic legacy

Historians still debate the economic legacy of the war. Some scholars believe that the war accelerated the pace of industrialization in the North. The demand for more and better weapons

Activists on a march during the Civil Rights movement of the 1950s and 1960s. They are demanding the rights of full citizenship that African Americans had theoretically been given at the end of the Civil War a century before, but that had never been properly protected.

21ST-CENTURY VIEW

At the beginning of the 21st century the legacies of the Civil War may have receded in the public's consciousness, but they have by no means disappeared. Books on the Civil War remain the single bestselling category of historical literature. Civil War novels such as Michael Shaara's *The Killer Angels* or Charles Frazier's *Cold Mountain* regularly top the bestseller lists of fictional works. Dozens of former Civil War battlefields have been preserved as state or national historical sites or parks, and they draw millions of visitors each year. Civil War reenactments have become a favorite pastime for thousands of Americans, who collect Civil War weapons, don authentic Confederate or Union uniforms, and replay major battles and even minor skirmishes. In the 1990s *The Civil War*, produced by Ken Burns, achieved record ratings for a TV documentary. It was rebroadcast in 2002 and attracted 27 million viewers.

A movement supporting government reparations for slavery has gained popularity in some segments of the African American community. Parents and educators continue to debate how slavery and the Civil War should be depicted in textbooks and at historic sites. Communities have been bitterly divided over such issues as whether monuments to slaveholders or Confederate leaders should be taken down or relabeled.

Supporters of the Democratic presidential candidate Bill Clinton at a rally in 1992. The U.S. political system has been dominated by Democrats and Republicans since the Civil War period.

and ammunition spurred innovations in manufacturing, and more Northerners left their farms and were exposed to life in the industrial workforce. Other experts, however, argue that the rapid growth in the wartime economy did not translate into permanent economic change in the postwar period. Wartime production was not particularly efficient, and the technologies developed for weaponry were not readily transferable to peacetime uses. In this view the war was an interruption in the ongoing industrialization of the United States. One thing seems certain, however: The effort to mobilize the economy to meet wartime demands contributed to an increase in the size and scale of industrial organizations. "Bigness" went on to become a hallmark of postwar corporate America.

A preview of modern warfare

Often referred to as the first modern war, the Civil War was one of the first large-scale conflicts in which the Industrial Revolution played a direct role in how the war was fought, as well as in its outcome. The war saw the first use of ironclad warships, submarines, aerial reconnaissance (balloons), and machine guns. The trench warfare that characterized the sieges of Petersburg and Richmond near the end of the war anticipated the tactics of World War I (1914–1918). For the first time railroads were used to move entire armies quickly to far-off battlefields. The telegraph kept distant commanders in communication with troops in the field. Mass production of factory-made weapons, ammunition, uniforms, and supplies played a crucial role in the Union's ultimate success.

Military strategy and tactics were forced to change to meet these new conditions. Union General William T. Sherman's march through Georgia and the Carolinas, which destroyed homes and farms and struck terror into civilians, previewed shock tactics that would be used in future wars. The size of Civil War armies and the casualties also foreshadowed a frightening future for warfare. Of the 2.5 million men who fought for the Union and 1 million who fought for the Confederacy 620,000 died in the war.

Cultural legacy

The Civil War left a deep cultural imprint on the United States. The exploits of the men in blue and gray have provided material for novelists, poets, historians, artists, and filmmakers. For many who participated in the war, it became the defining

episode of their lives, to be relived through Union and Confederate reunions and veterans' organizations well into the 20th century. For a generation or more, Civil War veterans dominated politics. In the South memories of the "Lost Cause" permeated popular culture. Movies and books with Civil War themes such as *Gone with the Wind* enjoyed huge popularity. Monuments honoring the dead were built throughout the country.

The legacy of the war is complex and evolving. The war unleashed historical forces that are still in motion today. Most importantly, the war brought slavery to an end. With emancipation Americans began an ongoing journey toward equality and true union. Historian Barbara Fields has said, "Without emancipation, the war was nothing but meaningless carnage."

Civil War veterans meet on the Bull Run (Manassas) battlefield in Virginia in 1881. Veterans dominated politics in the postwar decades.

See also

- Democratic Party
- Emancipation Proclamation
- Ku Klux Klan
- Literature
- Lost Cause
- March to the Sea and the Carolinas Campaign
- Memorials and souvenirs
- Movies
- National cemeteries
- Reconstruction
- Republican Party

Glossary

blockade-runner
A sailor or ship that broke through the Union blockade of Southern ports during the Civil War. Ships used in blockade-running were often specially built. They were fast and difficult to spot.

brevet rank
A promotion for an army officer to a higher rank, often as a honor just before retirement. There was no increase in pay and a limited increase in responsibilities.

brigade
A military unit consisting of between two and six regiments. The brigade was the common tactical unit of the Civil War.

casualty
A soldier lost in battle through death, wounds, sickness, capture, or missing in action. The huge number of casualties suffered by both sides during the Civil War—an estimated 620,000—was unprecedented.

commerce raider
A Confederate ship that targeted Union merchant shipping to undermine the North's ability to trade.

company
A military unit consisting of 50 to 100 men commanded by a captain. There were 10 companies in a regiment. Companies were raised by individual states.

conscription
Compulsory enrollment of able-bodied people into the armed forces, usually during a national emergency. Although unpopular, conscription was used by both the Union and the Confederacy.

corps
The largest military unit in the Civil War armies, consisting of two or more divisions. Corps were established in the Union army in March 1862 and in the Confederate army in November 1862.

division
The second largest military unit in the Civil War armies. A division was made up of three or four brigades and was commanded by a brigadier or major general. There were between two and four divisions in a corps.

habeas corpus
A legal protection against being imprisoned without trial. President Abraham Lincoln was severely criticized for suspending the right to trial in the Union during the war. President Jefferson Davis took a similar unpopular measure in the Confederacy.

mine
Known during the Civil War as "torpedoes," mines are explosive devices, usually concealed, designed to destroy enemy soldiers and transportation. Although considered at the time to be outside the bounds of acceptable warfare, they were used extensively in the Civil War.

mortar
A type of short-barreled cannon that threw shells in a high arc over enemy fortifications. They were usually used in siege warfare.

parole
Captured prisoners at the beginning of the war were exchanged and paroled, which meant they gave their word that they would not fight any more. The system became increasingly unworkable. Union authorities restricted the practice when they realized it was the main means by which the Confederacy replenished its troops.

partisan raiders
Irregular bands of troops, authorized by the Confederate government in April 1862 to operate behind enemy lines. They wore uniforms and were paid for captured war material they gave to the government. Despite some notable

successes, their overall usefulness to the Southern war effort has been disputed.

regiment
A military unit consisting of 10 companies of 100 men at full strength. In practice, however, most Civil War regiments were much smaller than this. Raised by state governors, they were usually composed of men from the same area. The Civil War soldier's main loyalty and sense of identity was connected to his regiment.

rifling
A technique used on both guns and cannons that allowed weapons to fire further and with greater accuracy than previously. Rifled barrels had spiral grooves cut into the inside, which gave a bullet or shell spin when fired.

secessionist
A person who supported the breaking away of the Southern states from the United States and thus a supporter of the Confederacy.

skirmishers
Infantrymen trained to fight in open order rather than the closed ranks of ordinary soldiers. They were often used ahead of the main force to prepare the way for a main attack or as snipers to harass an enemy counterattack.

sutler
A camp follower who sold provisions to the soldiers to supplement their army rations. Sutlers usually had a semi-official status and were attached to specific regiments. They were often resented for charging very high prices.

volunteer
A civilian who fights when his country goes to war, often because of personal convictions, a sense of adventure, or for a bounty or enlistment fee. The majority of Civil War soldiers were volunteers, rather than regular soldiers.

Further reading

Alleman, Tillie Pierce. *At Gettysburg, or What a Girl Saw and Heard of the Battle: A True Narrative.* New York: W. Lake Borland, 1889.

Berlin, Ira, et al. (editors). *Free at Last: A Documentary History of Slavery, Freedom, and the Civil War.* New York: The New Press, 1992.

Billings, John D. *Hardtack and Coffee, or the Unwritten Story of Army Life.* Boston: George M. Smith, 1887.

Bradford, Ned (editor). *Battles and Leaders of the Civil War.* New York: Dutton, 1956.

Catton, Bruce. *The Civil War.* Boston, MA: Houghton Mifflin, 1987.

Clark, Champ, and the editors of Time-Life Books. *The Assassination: Death of the President.* Alexandria, VA: Time-Life Books, 1987.

Coggins, Jack. *Arms and Equipment of the Civil War.* New York: Doubleday, 1962.

Damon, Duane. *When This Cruel War Is Over: The Civil War on the Home Front.* Minneapolis, MN: Lerner Publishing, 1996.

Engle, Stephen D. *The American Civil War: The War in the West 1861–July 1863.* London: Fitzroy Dearborn, 2001.

Evans, Charles M. *War of the Aeronauts.* Mechanicsburg, PA: Stackpole Books, 2002.

Faust, Patricia L. (editor). *Historical Times Illustrated Encyclopedia of the Civil War.* New York: Harper and Row, 1986.

Gallagher, Gary W. (editor). *The Wilderness Campaign.* Chapel Hill, NC: University of North Carolina Press, 1997.

Gallagher, Gary W. *The American Civil War: The War in the East 1861–May 1863.* London: Fitzroy Dearborn, 2001.

Gallagher, Gary W., and Robert Krick. *The American Civil War: The War in the East 1863–1865.* London: Fitzroy Dearborn, 2001.

Glatthaar, Joseph T. *The American Civil War: The War in the West 1863–1865.* London: Fitzroy Dearborn, 2001.

Grant, Ulysses S. *Personal Memoirs.* New York: Crescent Books, 1995.

Hendrickson, Robert. *The Road to Appomattox.* New York: John Wiley, 1998.

Kelbaugh, Ross J. *Introduction to Civil War Photography.* Gettysburg, PA: Thomas Publications, 1991.

McPherson, James M. *Battle Cry of Freedom.* New York: Oxford University Press, 1988.

Marrin, Albert. *Commander in Chief: Abraham Lincoln in the Civil War.* New York: Dutton, 1997.

Oates, Stephen B. *A Woman of Valor: Clara Barton and the Civil War.* New York: Macmillan/Free Press, 1994.

Robertson, James I. *Soldiers Blue and Gray.* Columbia, SC: University of South Carolina Press, 1998.

Schindler, Stanley (editor). *Memoirs of Robert E. Lee.* New York: Crescent Books, 1994.

Smith, Gene. *Lee and Grant: A Dual Biography.* New York: McGraw-Hill, 1984.

Trudeau, Noah. *Like Men of War: Black Troops in the Civil War, 1862–1865.* New York: Little, Brown, and Co, 1998.

Van Woodward, C. (editor). *Mary Chesnut's Civil War.* New Haven, CN: Yale University Press, 1981.

Wiley, Bell Irvin. *The Life of Johnny Reb: The Common Soldier of the Confederacy.* Baton Rouge, LA: Louisiana State University Press, 1980.

Wiley, Bell Irvin. *The Life of Billy Yank: The Common Soldier of the Union.* Baton Rouge, LA: Louisiana State University Press, 1981.

Wright, Mark. *What They Didn't Teach You about the Civil War.* Novato, CA: Presidio Press, 1996.

Useful websites:

These general sites have comprehensive links to a large number of Civil War topics:
http://sunsite.utk.edu/civil-war/warweb.html
http://civilwarhome.com/
http://americancivilwar.com/
http://www.civil-war.net/

http://www2.cr.nps.gov/abpp/battles/bystate.htm
This part of the National Parks Service site allows you to search for battles by state

http://pdmusic.org/civilwar.html
Sound files and words to Civil War songs

http://www.civilwarmed.org/
National Museum of Civil War Medicine

http://memory.loc.gov/ammem/aaohtml/exhibit/aopart4.html
Civil War section of the African American Odyssey online exhibition at the Library of Congress

http://valley.vcdh.virginia.edu/
The Valley of the Shadow Project: details of Civil War life in two communities, one Northern and one Southern

http://etext.lib.virginia.edu/civilwar/CivilWarBooks.html
Texts from the Civil War period online, including letters, poetry, and speeches

http://www.civilwarhome.com/records.htm
Battle reports by commanding generals from the Official Records

http://www.cwc.lsu.edu/
The United States Civil War Center at Lousiana State University

http://www.nps.gov/gett/getteducation/bcast20/act05.htm
Civil War slang

http://home.ozconnect.net/tfoen/
Original articles and images of the Civil War navies

http://civilwarmini.com/
Quizzes and interesting facts about the Civil War

Set Index

Page numbers in **bold** refer to volume numbers. Those in *italics* refer to picture captions, or where pictures and text occur on the same page.